How to Get
FREE
Stuff

with **Online Product Reviews**

**START FROM SCRATCH, BUILD A BRAND,
ATTRACT A SOCIAL FOLLOWING,
& GET A TON OF FREE STUFF**

TYLER CHRISTENSEN

TANAGER MEDIA PRESS

This was a boring page listing all of the legalese necessary so that nobody can get too mad at me if not all of their hopes and dreams come true. But all your hopes and dreams can come true, because you're awesome. So there's that.

Information about Tyler and Reviews of Cool Stuff can be found at the official website: www.reviewsofcoolstuff.com or on the official YouTube review channel at: http://www.youtube.com/c/ReviewsofCoolStuff

TABLE OF CONTENTS

PREFACE

How would you like to get free stuff?

Free stuff to wear. Free stuff to eat. Free stuff to play with. Free stuff that makes your household run more smoothly.

If you're like me, having the "brown Santa" (aka Amazon) drop packages off at your door everyday with useful stuff you want and need probably sounds like a pretty good idea.

And you can have that happen—for FREE!

Actually, that's not the whole truth. You might actually *get paid* to take, use, and keep that cool stuff. Pretty sweet, eh?

I first heard about product reviews about two years ago. The idea is that you write a review or promote a product on social media in exchange for a free or deeply discounted product.

What I heard is that it was super easy to get started doing these kinds of reviews (thanks McKay).

But without a social brand or audience of any kind, and without a lot of extra time to spend figuring out the whole online review thing I was skeptical. Even if I did have someone to pitch products to, I didn't have time to waste figuring this whole thing out.

However, with Christmas looming and with not enough gifts to feel happy about what I was providing for my family (I was unemployed at the time), I decided I should at least look into it. So I followed some links my little brother sent me and in just a few minutes created an online profile for one of the review companies he recommended (Tomoson).

Within a few days I received my first product, and it's been smooth sailing since then.

But let me back up and give you the whole story...

In 2016 I was a newly relocated and unemployed school teacher working a few part-time gigs from home while taking care of my four young children (ages 2-11). With a lot less money than we were accustomed to, it was a struggle to pay the bills, let alone get ahead on things. Everything was mostly fine, but with Christmas approaching I came to the sobering realization that while we still had a pretty great life, my kids would not be receiving many gifts for Christmas that year.

Now let me be clear, I don't spoil my kids and they would have been just fine getting nothing for Christmas as long as they got to spend the holiday together as a family (cue the "ahhhs"). But the primitive caveman provider in me wanted to give them more than just quality time with the family.

So I brainstormed different ways to make a few extra bucks and looked into several ways of getting free or deeply discounted products to give as gifts.

My little brother had been telling me for months that you can get cool free stuff simply by writing online reviews, but I had always brushed this off. However, now that I was in need he had my attention, so I gave him a call and got the skinny on how to be "an online influencer."

He recommended I pick a review company and complete my online profile. I picked Tomoson (www.tomoson.com)—the company he was using—and filled out my user profile. It only took a few minutes and was really easy to do. The problem I thought I would have is that I didn't have an online "brand" or any reason that influencers would want to work with me. Because of that I wasn't very hopeful that anyone would send me anything to review.

But I gave it a shot anyways, applying for stuff that I thought would be easy to get.

I applied for a few eBooks (not a physical product) and offered to make YouTube videos for a few of the lower-end products (like kitchenware, gardening tools, and winter gear).

I even applied for a few things I was interested in that cost money, but came at a deep discount.

After applying for 100 or so products I was surprised to find that companies were indeed willing to work with a nobody, and by Christmas time (less than a month) I had already received ten products for either deeply discounted prices or for free.

Pretty sweet.

Now fast forward to today.

In 2017 I "reviewed" a lot of cool stuff. And I mean A LOT! In my first 12 months as a reviewer/micro-influencer I received more than 400 total products with a total retail value of more than $5000.

Notice that I put "reviewed" in quotations. That is because for most of those products I did not actually have to write a review. Instead I simply took a picture and posted it on Twitter or Instagram (or both). You can see all of my posts at www.twitter.com/reviewsofcoolstuff and www.instagram.com/reviewsofcool.

By the end of 2017 several life changes had taken place in our home. By that point instead of under-employed I was actually over-employed, working 65-85 hours a week between three different jobs.

But here's the cool thing. I was (and am) still able to find time each week for posting my reviews. I've actually never had to spend more than five hours in a week doing reviews, and I usually only spend 1-2 hours each week (if that).

A typical week for me as a social influencer looks like this…

On Monday through Friday I spend a few minutes each morning applying for products I want on Tomoson, answering emails from people who find me through Amazon, YouTube, and Facebook, and some time ordering products.

This takes me 5-15 minutes each morning. Some weeks I don't do this until the weekend where I'll go through everything in about a half hour (applying for products and responding to emails).

Also, I used to spend an additional 5-10 minutes daily following and un-following people on social media, but now I mostly do that on the weekends, if at all... I have enough followers that I get accepted for a lot of products and I don't need to grow my audience to get cool stuff.

When I get home from work each day I'll see what the "brown Santa" (Amazon) has left for me and open it up and put it on my "to review" shelf. By the weekend I'll usually have anywhere from 10-20 items waiting to be reviewed. Most will be free products that simply require a photo or two. But I also get paid to post reviews.

Now that I have a sizeable audience on a few platforms many companies will pay me $3-7 to post a photo of one of their products with a short description and link to their product, or $15-25 to post a blog post or video review about their product. I make $50-200 each month with these kinds of posts.

I like to "batch" my posts—meaning that I save up the products and post a bunch of reviews at the same time.

On a typical Saturday I'll take pictures and maybe shoot a video or two. This usually takes just 5-10 minutes for shooting the pictures and videos and another 30-45 minutes to edit and post. I can usually knock all of those posts out in the same morning. If I have paid reviews (blog posts and YouTube videos) it will take me another hour or two.

Most weeks I get 10-15 products. And the vast majority of the products I receive to review are relatively cheap household or sporting good products, which are a cinch to "review." However, I also get 2-3 cool higher end products many weeks (like a drone, a massager, or a skateboard) and those reviews do take a little more time as they usually require a blog post and/or a YouTube video.

In all I'll spend 3-5 hours working on reviews each week and get paid a total of $25-50 weekly (in addition to keeping all the free products).

Pretty good gig, eh?

It really is pretty easy and the end result is amazing, so I want you to learn how to do it. In this book I will tell you everything that I did to get set up with a reviewing company, how to build a social media brand from scratch, how to become an influencer on those channels, and how to get a ton of FREE stuff.

Giddy-up.

CHAPTER 1:

What is social influence?

Let's start with the basics. What is social influence?

A simple definition might be "the influence for change that one person has on another." (I put that definition in quotation marks which generally means you're quoting someone or something, but I'm just quoting myself... I simply wanted it to look official).

So what does social influence have to do with getting products?

Social marketing is one of the main marketing channels today. In the past you could get your product out to the masses by putting an ad on a Super Bowl commercial, or by purchasing space in a magazine or newspaper. Or you could make a radio commercial or put up a billboard. The problem with those "traditional" methods is that they are all pretty

1

expensive, so you need to have considerable moolah in order to advertise.

It's a little different today. Actually it's a LOT different. Good products can be and often are promoted using word-of-mouth advertising.

Word-of-mouth or social marketing has been around forever. But it used to occur mostly when somebody liked something and they told others about it. As word spread more and more people would purchase that product based on its reputation.

Today this word-of-mouth marketing often occurs through the use of social media. When somebody likes something today they can tell a friend OR they can post it on their Facebook wall, Tweet about it, share pictures on Instagram, or even make a YouTube video. And any of these methods have the potential to go viral, which can result in huge exposure and consequent sales.

So smart businesses today use traditional advertising methods AND take advantage of word-of-mouth or social marketing utilizing various social channels. Social marketing can be very cost effective—especially for smaller businesses—and it is relatively easy to do. Companies just need freelancing "social influencers" to spread the word.

This is where you come in.

You can be a social influencer that helps different companies share their products with the world.

You can be a freelancer—someone who works as an independent contractor (is unaffiliated with any particular company)—and promote products for dozens (or even hundreds) of different companies.

But what if you aren't currently a social influencer? What if you don't even have any social media accounts or a large social following? What if you've never partnered with or created relationships with any company or brand?

No problem.

You're in the right place. In this chapter I'll go over what social influencers do, what kind of influence they can have, and why you should become a social influencer—even if you currently have no social presence at all.

3

Getting Started

When I began this journey into social marketing I had no idea how to cultivate a following. I was simply a regular guy who wanted to get free stuff.

Indeed, I never viewed myself as a "social influencer", mostly because I had no idea what a social influencer was. Sure, I knew that celebrities could influence others to make shopping decisions, but I had no idea that regular people could wield social influence, and I hadn't the foggiest notion of how to get others to follow me on my social channels.

But that is exactly what needs to happen if you want to get cool stuff for free. Sure, you can get some stuff without having a large following online, but the best stuff is reserved for those who have a substantial following.

Why?

Because that is how the companies and brands benefit from working with freelancers (aka "regular people"). Smart companies give freelancers something for free, and in return they ask them to share their product with the freelancer's audience, which they hope will result in more sales of their product.

In the case of affiliate marketing (more about that in chapter three) both the freelancer and the company make money, so it's definitely a winning proposition.

Brands want to work with social influencers because it's an easy and cost effective way of increasing brand awareness, generating new and more traffic to their site, increasing user engagement, and boosting overall sales.

And freelancing social influencers want to work with companies because that's how they get cool stuff for free (or even get paid to promote).

Micro, Macro, & Mega Influencers

So if you want to get free stuff you need to become a social influencer. But there are several different kinds of influencers, including micro, macro, and mega influencers. Which kind should you become?

Let me explain…

Micro-influencers are social influencers with an audience of 10k to 100k followers (or possibly even less).

They are in the hobby phase of promoting products and can get deeply discounted or free products for lower-end merchandise. These influencers create relationships with brands and companies that can become very significant down the road but with a small audience micro-influencing freelancers probably won't get rich in this phase.

Micro-influencers that get deals tend to have a very targeted audience, so if the niche you are interested in lines up closely with any particular brand, this can be a match made in influencer heaven. At this micro level it is important that you have high engagement with your audience, that your posts are being liked, shared and retweeted, and that the links are being clicked.

As a micro-influencer your selling proposition to any company should be that your audience is definitely interested in their product, and that if you share it with your followers they will buy it. And if you get brand deals, do whatever you can to deliver on that promise. Write good copy, post amazing pictures, shoot great videos, and help your audience see why they should make a purchase.

Any success you have as a micro-influencer will propel you towards a larger platform and ultimately help you to become a macro or mega influencer.

The micro stage of influence is likely where you currently are or where you hope to be in the short-term.

Brands want to work with micro-influencers because while their audiences are relatively small, there is often a high level of engagement between the influencer and their followers. And that's your pitch to these companies… "work with me and trust me, my followers will want your product." You need to sell them on your ability to get their product in front of a warm audience.

Many companies love working with micro-influencers because there is very little risk and little cost. And this is great for freelancers like you because becoming a micro-influencer has a very low barrier for entry.

Being a micro influencer is a great entry point for people who want free stuff—even if they have little to no brand of their own—because companies are willing to take a chance on an unknown freelance influencer because of the potential upside.

7

So become a micro influencer.

It doesn't take much. Set up a few social profiles (on Twitter, Facebook, Instagram, etc.) and then start reaching out to companies (more about this later). Then, after you've started making and posting reviews, your own reputation and brand will grow and before you know it you'll be positioned to become a macro-influencer.

Macro-influencers are typically those who have an audience of 100k to several million. These influencers are often minor web celebrities or highly respected content creators that have grown their audiences considerably over time. Macro influencers almost always start out as micro-influencers.

Much like micro-influencers, macro-influencers typically have a strong connection with their audience and tend to have high engagement on their various social channels. Unlike micro-influencers, however, macro-influencers are the trendsetters that make a real impact on who likes (and buys) things online.

While a general rule of thumb is that to be a macro influencer you need to have an audience size of 100k or more, the actual size of a macro-influencer's audience depends upon the platform. For example, on Instagram an influencer reaches macro status at about 100k followers. However, on YouTube and Facebook one probably needs 250k followers or more to be considered a macro influencer.

With social media, benchmarks and expectations for influencers continue to change and evolve. And as new platforms are created and grow in popularity, it is imperative that macro-influencers make the necessary adjustments.

 Once trending Vine and Snapchat celebrities have had to find new platforms since their main platforms declined in popularity, while YouTubers have had to adjust to algorithmic changes on the YouTube platform.

While micro-influencers are building an audience and aren't likely to get rich from social media, macro-influencers already have a large audience so their earnings potential is much much higher.

A macro-influencer can make money through advertising, affiliate marketing, and getting paid directly from the brands that they represent and promote.

And the pay can be really good.

In 2016, a survey by later.com showed that the average price paid for an Instagram post to an influencer with an audience of over one million on Instagram was more than $6000. For influencers with 200k-500k followers the payment was just under $2000, and for influencers with less than 200k followers the post was worth less than $1,000.

Many macro-influencers make enough money from doing product reviews so that building a brand becomes their full-time profession and income.

If this is appealing to you, start with the brand and audience that you have and then grow it. This will take a lot of work and you'll need to do something to differentiate yourself from all the other YouTube and Insta-Celebs out there. It can be done, it just requires a lot of hard work.

Mega influencers (e.g. Kim Kardashian, Beyoncé, etc.) have millions of followers but rarely have high engagement with those followers—it's simply too difficult at that scale.

If you're reading this you are not a mega influencer and you probably will never be one, so don't worry about it.

Brand Ambassadors

The goal of an influencer—whether they be micro-, macro-, or a mega-influencer—is to "influence" a potential customer to purchase a product. And an influencer can do this having never tried the product themselves. Influencers are salespeople, but not necessarily endorsers.

What makes an "ambassador" different from other influencers is that they have tried and love the product they are promoting. Often these are users who love a product and will promote it—even if they are not paid for doing so.

A good brand ambassador will have a large audience, understand general marketing principles, be committed to building and growing relationships, and be professional.

Obviously, this is the kind of influencer and partner that companies love to have. If your reviews come from your own experience with the product, that experience will give you so much more "social proof" or credibility with your audience, and that will almost always convert better (get more sales) than simply advertising the product.

11

Like I mentioned earlier some brand ambassadors are paid while others are not. If you aren't "paid" as a brand ambassador, why become one?

There are actually a few reasons, and some of them do involve getting paid.

First, because you love the product. If you're hanging out in the review space you really should be promoting your favorite products, even if you aren't getting paid for those reviews. Treat this as an opportunity as a raving fan to practice writing review and sales copy.

You should also endorse products because it helps you to create important relationships. If you're giving mad props to a company over an extended period of time, they might reach out to you with free products or samples so that you can continue promoting them.

Or you can reach out to them. I've done this with a few companies, sending a simple email that basically says "I love your stuff and rave about it online on these social media channels and through reviews. If you ever have new products that you'd like me to test out, I'd be happy to help." And I've gotten some cool free stuff this way.

Finally, you should become a brand ambassador because this is a great way to get into the influencer and marketing space. If you are new to writing product reviews, this is a great way for you to start.

I started writing Amazon reviews for everything I bought part way through 2017. Within six months I was a top reviewer on Amazon with a review rank in the top 10k and at one year I was in the top 1,000.

At that point I started getting dozens of emails every week from companies that hoped I would review their products. Most were simply willing to send me a free product, but there were several that were also willing to pay for reviews.

This gets into gray area regarding Amazon's terms of service and I'll cover it in greater detail in Chapter Three. For now, just know that becoming a brand ambassador and reviewing your favorite products is a great idea.

When you are a brand ambassador you will have all sorts of different ways to grow and monetize your own personal brand.

What kind of influencer will you be?

If you are just starting out than a reasonable short-term goal is to become a micro-influencer that is growing and cultivating a targeted audience.

Be someone who helps brands get the word out and build their businesses. You can always become a larger influencer or a brand ambassador at some point down the road once you've created relationships with various companies and brands.

Perhaps the greatest benefit of starting with the goal of becoming a micro-influencer is that as a smaller influencer you will be able to learn about your industry while getting free products and affiliate deals.

There's no need to wait.

Then, as you learn more about being an influencer you can grow into a larger influencer role in a more targeted niche or area. And you can start making money doing reviews.

My own experience has shown me how valuable it is to start small. In my first year as an influencer I learned that there are certain categories of products that were super easy to get accepted for product reviews. For me these included things like book reviews, kitchen items, bicycling gear, and small Bluetooth speakers and power banks.

As a micro-influencer I quickly had to decide which products were worth my time to review. While everyone is willing to send free books in exchange for reviews, I didn't have or want to make the time needed to do book reviews.

So I didn't.

And after receiving dozens of speakers, headphones, and watches I decided I didn't really need more of those (or particularly like reviewing them), so I stopped.

On the other hand I found that while I personally don't really care for remote controlled drones, they make killer gifts so I still apply for and receive drones to review (I've reviewed 10-15 of them already even though this isn't' my primary niche).

I started with no brand, no social media, no following of any sort. But I started small and built up an audience while I did those early reviews. I also got better at reviews and started creating more professional review videos and higher quality picture posts. I'm not quite to the macro level yet, but I do have an established brand so I get dozens of requests for reviews each month and now most of those reviews are paying me in addition to sending the free product.

Now that I've grown my social following to over 50k I can certainly be a little pickier and more targeted in my reviews, going after higher end electronics and toys.

I also now feel like more of a pro and have had to spend time creating a media kit and developing my own brand (more about that later). Transitioning from micro- to macro-influencer is a lot of fun and makes the early reviews more than worth the time.

CHAPTER 2

How to Get Cool Stuff

So you've decided this sounds like a pretty good gig and you'd like to be an influencer. But how do you get cool stuff to review in the first place?

That's pretty simple. You just need to ask.

And the first thing you need to know about asking for free stuff online is that the more you ask the more you get (both in terms of quantity and quality).

As an influencer (or a potential influencer) brands want to know who you are and what you can do for them. You make their job easier by letting them know just that.

Contact the companies you are interested in and let them know what you are willing to do to promote their brand.

How are brands promoted online by micro-influencers?

Companies big and small love when their products are shared by word-of-mouth. So, like I explained in Chapter one if you share a brand or company's product with your friends and followers that is a great (and cheap) way for that company to do advertising.

Brands are also looking for high quality demonstrations or tutorials of customers using or installing their products. They place these videos on YouTube or on Amazon to help those who are searching for theirs or similar products gain a better understanding of how the products work and why they should buy them.

These videos can gain organic traffic—or traffic that comes from search. So even if you don't have any audience, a brand might want to work with you if you can create something that fills a need.

Think about it. Is it more cost effective to hire a large firm to create an unboxing or demo video for several thousand dollars, or to hire several micro-influencers to do the same thing in exchange for the product or for a small fee?

It's really a no-brainer.

Companies and brands are in the business of making money and if you can show them how you can help in that area they will be willing and anxious to work with you.

So you need to develop the skill of advertising products and then companies will want to give you free stuff to review.

Getting FREE stuff to Review

There are a number of ways to get free stuff to review, but all of them involve doing something. Whether that be creating a social post (Twitter, Instagram, or Facebook), making an unboxing or demonstration video on YouTube, or writing an in-depth blog post or review. Each of these activities takes time and some skill (though most can be easily learned).

Social posts are the easiest to create as often all they require is a photo and a link to their Amazon listing. However, what does take time is building up the social brand and acquiring followers. Ideally this would be somewhat organic with you gaining consistently more followers the more you review.

A social post can be created and poosted in as little as 1-2 minutes. You simply take a picture of the product, write a short 10-30 word description of the product, maybe throw in a few hashtags or keywords, and finally add a link to the purchase page.

Most of my "reviews" are actually just social posts, and I can do as many as 20 in a week without spending more than an hour or two of my own time. This is a great way to get free stuff without having to spend a lot of time.

Unboxing, demonstration, and how-to tutorial videos take a little more time, but they too can be very worthwhile as a product reviewer. If you are accepted for an advertising campaign that involves video it is probably because the brand or company needs customer testimonials on how awesome their product is.

Unboxing videos are very popular right now on YouTube, while demonstration videos can be posted on YouTube or directly on the Amazon product page. Tutorials can be used on the company websites or across social channels.

The best thing about making videos is that as you get better at it you'll be able to create videos that cover all these different areas and can be used in multiple places. For example, you may do a short unboxing and testimonial of a product and then conclude the video with a demonstration or tutorial. That video can then be placed on YouTube, Facebook, and Amazon and be linked to or embedded on Twitter and Instagram.

Finally, *blog posts or actual reviews and/or testimonials* can be very valuable to brands and companies. If you write about your experience on a blog post you can utilize your other kinds of posts (picture and videos) to enhance and deepen the review.

So a blog post might show several pictures, have an embedded tutorial video, and also include a written description of the benefits of the product.

These kinds of posts are super valuable to companies but are also a LOT of work for influencers. Indeed, I only do a blog post now if a company is willing to pay me a reasonable sum for doing so.

Speaking of getting paid…

Getting Paid for Reviews

If you play your cards right, not only will you start getting stuff for free (in exchange for a review or social post), you can also GET PAID to make those reviews and posts.

That's right, someone may be willing to pay you to take their stuff.

Influencer companies like Tomoson actually advertise paid reviews, so you can apply for those kinds of reviews and if you have the right kind of following with a large enough audience you will be selected for paid reviews.

For me this actually was much easier and happened much sooner than I expected. I started doing reviews in December 2016 and I got my first paid review on Tomoson just four months later—I was paid $25 to write a blog post about a Mandolin slicer.

At the time I only had about 10k twitter followers and 6k Instagram followers, with just a handful of followers on Facebook and less than 1,000 total views on my blog. But I must have offered a cheaper post than others because I was selected for the campaign.

Since then I have tinkered around with applications and have found a sweet spot on what I charge for paid reviews, whether it be an Instagram post, a Twitter post, a blog post, or a YouTube video (usually an unboxing video).

I made just shy of $1000 doing paid reviews in my first year, mostly through $5 Instagram posts that literally took less than five minutes each to create and post.

As my brand and audience has grown my rates have gone up so now I get paid a little more for each review so I can spend less total time reviewing but make even more money.

And while most of my earliest paid reviews were for social posts on Instagram, now most of my paid reviews come through YouTube, even though I have less than 200 subscribers. I think it is because my videos have improved and some of them have several thousand views (so I have proof that they reach their intended audience).

You can check out my YouTube reviews at: http://youtube.com/reviewsofcoolstuff. My channel has two parts—the biggest part contains all my video reviews of various products. But I also have several videos on how to make good review videos and improve your social media profile and brand, so check it out if you want to get more followers and grow your brand.

There are also companies that will pay you to do what they call "content distribution." That means they will provide you the images and the text for your post, and you simply have to post it for them to your audience.

In my experience companies are most interested in doing these kinds of posts before holiday sales or other giveaway type situations in order to build brand recognition. No matter the reason, it is cool too get paid for seconds of work.

With content distribution I charge the same amount as my other posts but content distribution posts are even easier to do and faster to post (in some cases you just click the "post" button and it automatically attaches their text and photos) to your social post. I've made as much as $35 for doing this.

These kinds of posts are great to get, but you may not get them right away. Be patient and build your brand and then they'll start coming.

Companies that exchange products for reviews (Where to find products to review)

So where do you go to get hooked up with free products?

There are tons of companies out there that connect reviewers to the companies that need products reviewed. Simply Google something like "review products for free" and you're bound to get a long list of companies that would love to work with you.

In 2019 some of the bigger more established companies include:

Tomoson – This is the first company I started working with and I still do a lot of my reviews through them. They have all kinds of different products and unlike most of the other review sites they offer a lot of paid reviews in addition to exchanging reviews for free and heavily discount products.

Snagshout – The let you redeem a "snag" every three days. Most of the products are deeply discounted but not free and they don't offer paid reviews.

Vipon – One of the older review sites, Vipon was previously known as AMZ Review Trader.

Influenster – This site connects reviewers with products in the hair, makeup, and beauty space. It also has other products, but the focus is definitely on personal appearance.

Reviews 4 Success – This site is another one that will send you various kinds of products and if you have a large enough audience you can get paid reviews for your posts.

There are tons of social channels you might use for your reviews, but if you're starting from scratch you probably want to go with the social channels that you are most familiar with and where you have the largest audience.

Whether that be Facebook, Twitter, Instagram, Pinterest, YouTube or some other social channel… if you are willing to post and promote, someone will be more than happy to give you free or discounted products.

In the next chapter I will walk you through how to maximize your profile in each of these social channels and build up your audience.

Amazon Reviews

When you start receiving products from different companies it is a really good idea to do reviews for those products on Amazon. I wish I had learned this lesson earlier.

When you review products on Amazon those reviews contribute to your reviewer rank. If you are a highly ranked reviewer than many people will start reaching out to you to review their products.

There is a lot of gray area when it comes to Amazon reviews. Amazon wants honest reviews so that the reviews are actually helpful in the purchasing process. Unfortunately there are a lot of people out there getting paid to do reviews, so in some cases even if a product is really horrible it may have several five-star reviews written by people who don't even own the product and/or who were bribed to write good reviews.

Amazon has done a few things to discourage these types of reviews. In early 2017 they started making a distinction between "verified" and "non-verified" reviews.

When I first started doing product reviews I posted Amazon reviews only for the reviews that I included in my blog, and I only did that because I could copy and paste the reviews from the blog into Amazon.

At the beginning of the year my Amazon reviewer rank was number 2.2 million. But with the handful of Amazon reviews I posted each month my rank started steadily climbing. Six months after I start post reviews my rank had moved up to 122,000 and at that point I decided to start doing more Amazon reviews for products that I really liked. I set the goal to improve my rank to the top 20,000 by the end of the year.

With that goal I started doing Amazon reviews for any product I received and liked that had less than ten total reviews. If it was a nicer (i.e. tech) product I even included video reviews (usually unboxing) in hopes of getting more "helpful" votes.

Posting more reviews paid off. I cracked the top 10,000 towards the end of my first year doing reviews and started getting 2-3 daily emails from brands that found me on Amazon because of my high ranking.

Most of those brands offered to send me things I didn't want, but there were a few each week that sent me great products. I got drones, skateboards, massagers, and other cool things and wrote really good reviews for those products.

Unfortunately I was a casualty of the "Great Amazon Purge of 2017." Just after cracking the top 1,000 reviewers, all of my reviews (by then I had a few hundred) were deleted and my reviewing privileges were revoked.

I felt I had been playing by the book so I reached out several times to Amazon to see what I had done wrong and to see if their decision to ban me could be reversed. I was never given a response and my posting privileges were never restored.

Would I still do Amazon reviews if I had to start over?

Yes. My one year doing Amazon reviews resulted in me getting a ton of great products and motivated me to improve my reviews, videos, and photos. I have a stronger brand because of it. And I continue to get requests for reviews from people who found me through Amazon or a list of top reviewers of Amazon from months ago when I was highly ranked.

In short, Amazon gave me opportunities to reach more people. It's a bummer I was banned, especially as nearly every reviewer in the top 1,000 was/is doing reviews just like I was (getting free or reduced prices on products in exchange for reviews). That's how you make it to the top 1,000. Sometimes it works and sometimes it doesn't. You just need to roll with the punches and take advantage of whichever platform is working for you.

Also, I just recently learned about the Amazon Influencer Program. This is the official Amazon channel for getting products and reviewing them. I saw an ad for the program and decided to check it out even though I was banned from doing reviews.

Turns out that if you have a brand with enough followers, they let you in. My application took ten minutes and because I have enough followers on Twitter and Instagram I was immediately accepted into the program.

So now I have my very own Amazon storefront at: https://www.amazon.com/shop/reviewsofcoolstuff and I can make money from affiliate links on that page. I can also do reviews again through Amazon using my branded channel instead of my personal account.

Amazon has options… but they are in control. I'm a little wary of investing too much time and attention into doing Amazon reviews again because I could get banned and have to start over.

Fortunately Amazon isn't the only place where you can get exposure so that people will find you to do reviews (and get paid for those reviews).

Facebook Groups

There are tons of different online groups and communities that promote and support online reviews. Pick any social network and search for "online reviews" and you are sure to come up with dozens of groups.

I have found that Facebook in particular, has a strong community supporting and soliciting online reviews. If you search for and join these groups you will get onto the radar of many different companies and brands that need help with reviewing products. And as you review their products they will share your information with others who will request to "become your friend" on Facebook.

But beware, once you go down this rabbit hole it isn't so easy to come back.

I was amazed at the bombardment of friend requests I got after doing a couple of reviews for companies I found (or that found me) on Facebook. I got a few requests my first week, several more the second, and then tons each week after that.

I was able to get some cool products through "friends" who found me on Facebook, added me to their list of reviewers, and shared that list with their other collaborators.

As someone who likes to keep my personal and business lives separate this became an issue for me.

Ultimately, despite reviewing several really cool products that I found on Facebook groups, I decided to "unfriend" all of my business connections on Facebook and go a different route. It just wasn't worth having my Facebook account being overrun by review solicitors.

I will still occasionally get new friend requests or even messages on FB messenger from non-friends and sometimes still check them out.

If there is something I really want I'll go ahead and respond and do the review. Only a few of these Facebook reviews have been paid reviews, and almost all of them want Amazon reviews in exchange for a product.

So you'll have to play it by ear and see what they have to offer on Facebook groups. You may decide this is a great way to get leads and create relationships with companies. Or you may decide like I have that there are other platforms that are better suited to how you work and what you want to accomplish.

I'm currently working on building up my YouTube channel so when I get review requests from people who found me on Amazon or through Facebook I often ignore the requests. They are usually for products I am not interested in and I don't want/need to forge a relationship with those companies.

But I'm always on the lookout for good partners. If there is something offered that I actually do want I ask if they'll be happy with a YouTube unboxing instead of an Amazon review in exchange for the product and many companies will agree to that.

Which is fantastic because I have found that YouTube has been a great platform for me to use for reviews and to get leads for new products to review.

YouTube

I feel I need to put a quick plug in for YouTube here—even though I'll be discussing this platform more in Chapter Three—because I have been surprised by how many companies and sellers have found and reached out to me via my contact information found on YouTube.

I have grown my YouTube platform very slowly. I started making reviews with absolutely no knowledge or experience in creating videos and I was happy to only spend an hour or two each week doing online reviews, so making fancy videos was never a priority.

However, I have found that with each new video that I create for YouTube I am getting better as a reviewer and I am growing my audience—both for people who want to buy the products I am reviewing, as well as for companies who want to work with me. I now get many requests each week to create YouTube videos.

YouTube is a great platform for product reviews because it allows you to actually show the benefits of the product you are reviewing. There are three primary ways to do a review on YouTube—an unboxing, a demonstration, and a product review.

Unboxing videos. An unboxing video is one where you simply take the product out of the box or wrapping while talking about the features offered by the product.

These videos are pretty easy to make, just read the product description on Amazon or the company's website and maybe read a few Amazon reviews prior to unboxing. Then, reiterate what you read while you take it out of the box.

I can prep for an unboxing in 5-10 minutes, take 2-3 minutes to shoot the film, and spent almost no time editing. So the entire video can be created and uploaded to YouTube in 30 minutes or less.

I typically charge $15-25 for an unboxing video, or may do them for free if I really want the product. But even the videos that I make for free will sometimes bring me money. In the next chapter I'll discuss how you can make money on YouTube will affiliate sales and advertising revenue.

Demonstration videos. A demonstration video is one where you show your audience how to use the product, install the product, etc. These can be really helpful videos for potential customers and can be great for you too because people will watch them now and in the future.

Demo videos take a little more time to make because you have to shoot "B-roll", which is essentially photos and videos that show the product in use and/or stock photography showing off key features of the product. On these videos you probably won't do straight shots but instead piece together several clips and add a voice-over track.

I typically charge $25-50 for a demonstration video. Demos and how-tos are my most trafficked videos on YouTube because once the rush of purchasing a new product is over people want to know how to use or install that product. So these videos get a bump around the holidays (when people are buying them) but also get plenty of views during the rest of the year as people are figuring out how to use them.

Product Review videos. A product review video can be a very detailed review based on your own experience and/or recap others experience with the product. These videos can include demonstrations and how-tos, but don't necessarily have to. The key is to find out what the company wants and expects from you and to create your video accordingly.

If you do a simple product review video you can find most or all of the information needed for the video from Amazon reviews, the product page, and the actual product packaging. With that information just explain the features of the product in your video. You can throw in little details about the product if you've actually been using it for a while, but that isn't necessary—you can simply share what others have said.

This type of product review is simple and only takes 5-10 minutes of preparation and another few minutes to shoot and edit. I typically charge $15-30 for a simple product review video.

However, you can also make much more detailed product review videos that include your own experience AND a product demonstration or how-to.

That kind of review video takes a little more work (it's essential an unboxing and a demonstration video) and I charge about double ($30-65) to create those videos UNLESS

I really want the product and/or I think I can make a lot of money off affiliate sales.

This leads me to an important note about YouTube videos. You can make as much or more money after the video is posted through YouTube ads (if you have enough subscribers to monetize) or affiliate sales.

I have several products that I reviewed for free that bring me a few dollars each month from advertising (they get a lot of views) and a few dollars each month from affiliate sales. I'll explain more about affiliate marketing in chapter five. Regardless of what type of video you choose to create on YouTube, YT can be an important platform for you to grow and market your brand. As you gain views and subscribers you become more and more attractive to companies looking for influencers.

And as your channel and brand grow you will find companies reaching out to you to market their products, you will get better products to review, and you'll be able to increase the price you charge to review those products. For these reasons I recommend getting started with video reviews ASAP.

So if you're getting started as a product reviewer and social influencer you can get products by reaching out to companies directly and through various websites that connect brands with influencers (e.g. Tomoson). Pretty soon you'll have companies find and reach out to you through Amazon, Facebook, and YouTube.

However, in order to be attractive to these companies you need to have a solid brand with an audience that wants those products. In the next chapter I will walk you through the steps required to build a brand and grow a following.

CHAPTER 3

Building a Brand

So now that you know how and where to find products that companies will send you for free, it is important that you create the sort of online profile that appeals to these brands and companies. You do that by setting up your own blog or website, establishing various social channels, and then by attracting followers to those channels.

The good news is that setup for all of these platforms is relatively easy and you can do it in a day or a weekend.

Creating a blog or Website

While it is possible to create a brand and get free stuff without a website, it is infinitely easier with one. And fortunately we live in a time where websites can be created easily, in little time, and for little or no money.

Lucky! (said in my best Napoleon Dynamite voice)

The benefit of having your own website is that it gives you more control over your brand, it creates a home base for promoting and selling products, and provides you with a space to advertise and promote yourself as an influencer.

If you don't already have a site you have essentially three options:

1) go free
2) pay a little bit and do most or all of the work yourself
3) pay someone else to create a professional site.

I recommend you go with option no. 1 first (the free option) to get your feet wet, then upgrade to no. 2 (pay a little) within your first year.

If your brand really grows to the point you're making serious income then consider going to no. 3 (a paid site).

Let me walk you through each of these three options.

Option No. 1: Create a Free Website

It's true, you can have your very own FREE website in ten minutes or less. Here are a few of the advantages and disadvantages of creating a free site.

Advantages of creating a free site:
- It's free
- It takes very little time to get a site up-and-running
- You can create as many websites as you want
- You don't have to worry about purchasing and managing your domain name and website host

Disadvantages of creating a free site:
- You don't own the domain name, but must use a subdomain associated with your chosen platform (e.g. www.wix.com/reviewsofcoolstuff)
- You have limited control over the look of the site (e.g. themes, plugins)
- You have limited options for search engine optimization (more about this later)
- Someone else "owns" your site. If they decide to close up shop, start charging for use, etc. then you have limited options

We now live in a time where there is no excuse for not having a website. You can literally create one FOR FREE in ten minutes or less. Simply go to one of the free platforms by searching "free website." The most popular platforms right now are Wix, Weebly, and Yola.

Go to your chosen platform and follow the instructions they give you to set up a site. Most free sites are "drag-and-drop" so you'll create your site simply by choosing the colors, themes, and features that you want.

It's so easy that I actually recommend you do it RIGHT NOW (it'll take like five minutes).

Are you back already? Easy, right?

Now try building the same site on two or three different platforms to see which one you like best. (So if you created you first site on Wix, now try to create one with the same information on Weebly).

This exercise (of creating multiple free websites) is worth an hour or two of your time because the result is that you will then have several websites and can pick the site that you like the most to start promoting your products and your services as a reviewer. And you can easily delete all the other websites you don't need.

Remember, with a free website you are limited in what you can create but you also can easily delete and start over if you don't like what you have.

Option No. 2: Create a Paid (but Inexpensive) Site

After you've played around with one or more free sites you'll probably have a much better sense of what you want to include on your site and what limitations you have by sticking with the free option.

So you may want to upgrade to a paid site. And the good news is that a paid site doesn't have to be expensive.

However, there are several different components to owning your own website (hosting, domain, themes and plugins). Let me walk you through a few of these things.

Hosting. Your biggest cost will be for "hosting" the website. That is—the company you use that will put all your files on their web servers so that the world can see your site.

This will likely run you about $5/month or $50-100/year, but you can find some really good deals by locking into a company for a year or two.

Some of the big web hosting companies include GoDaddy, Blue Host, and Host Gator, but you can find a great host by simply Googling "cheap web hosts" and reading a few reviews or looking at comparison sites. Some of these hosts are as cheap as $1/month for hosting.

And here's a pro tip: Any time you buy any sort of technology resource online (including hosting, domains, themes and plugins) don't pay full price for it. There are so many online discounts and coupons available if you simply search for them.

For example, if you need web hosting and have decided to go through Go Daddy... Simply google "Go Daddy coupon code web hosting" and see what pops up.
It is likely that you'll be able to get all of your tech needs covered with at least a 25-50% discount.

Domain. On top of hosting you'll need to purchase your domain name. Just go to a website that handles domain registration (this includes sites like www.godaddy.com or www.googledomains.com) and pick one out.

A domain will cost you about $15/year depending on who you go with for a dot com. And of course you can add the search term "discount or coupon code" to get that domain as a steep discount—at least for the first year.

You might try searching something like "GoDaddy domain discount code 2019" for best results. You are sure to find some online code that will at least save you a few bucks.

Themes and Plugins. Finally, while you can get a theme (the overall design template) for free to start you will probably eventually want to pony up a one-time expense of $25-100 to purchase a premium theme so that your website looks better (and different from) your competitors. A good theme will also make it easier to make updates to the site, allowing you to spend your extra time writing not designing.

You can find themes at Theme Forest, Colorlib, or by searching "Wordpress themes". And you don't need to pay for a theme right away, go ahead and experiment with one of thousands of FREE themes until you get a sense of how you want your site to look.

You can always purchase a premium theme later. And don't forget to search for coupon codes when you do purchase a theme. And getting that discount should be a "theme" that you see developing here in this chapter—you can always get online discounts for digital products.

Plugins are another expense that you'll eventually want but probably don't need in the very beginning.

A plugin is something that helps your website do something that it can't do by default. So if you want to sell something, collect email addresses, or have a fancier contact form or something like that you'll need to download a plugin.

The good news is that most plugins are free and they are easy to find by simply going to the "add plugin" portion of your WordPress dashboard. A theme with some basic plugins is all you need to start laying out your website.

Once you've established a web host, purchased your domain name, and set up your theme and plugins you are ready to launch your very own website. At this point it's all about content creation.

Creating Good Content. Start by creating a home page, an about page, and probably a contact form. And that is probably all you need to get started.

All in (on the option. No. 2—paid site) you'll probably spend $100-150 for your first year (including set-up costs) and $50-100 each year thereafter. Not bad to have a cool website, but not worth it if you aren't making money with your reviews yet. That's why option no.1 exists.

With such a small startup cost you will probably want to upgrade (from free to paid) at some point. Here are some of the advantages and disadvantages of paying for your own website:

Advantages of a paid (but inexpensive) site:
- You have more options for how it looks
- You gain more control over your brand (important for scaling up and making money)
- You have a dedicated URL or web address (e.g. www.reviewsofcoolstuff.com)
- By creating the site yourself you gain the skill of "website design", a skill that will improve your reviews and could even make you money as a freelancer.

Disadvantages of a paid (but inexpensive) site:

- It takes a little time to set up (probably 10 hours or more to do it right)
- It costs a little bit of money
- If you haven't done anything like this before there is a little bit of a learning curve (but honestly, it's not very hard—just Google anything you get stuck on).

As you look over this list of advantages and disadvantages it should be exceedingly clear that taking the time to create your own website is not only doable but in your best interest. Don't stress if you feel you can't do this right away.

Start with a free site and when you feel up to it start creating your own site. You can take as much time as you need.

It's worth the small amount of time and money needed to make this happen. Creating your own site may seem overwhelming but every aspect of the setup and design is readily available on YouTube, just search and you'll find dozens of videos about the process.

When it comes to your brand you should be in the driver seat, and creating your own website will put you there.

Option No. 3: Hire a Professional to Build your Site

As your brand grows you might get to the point where you want to invest in hiring a professional web designer.

Having someone else work on your site will free up your time to work on other aspects of the business and will hopefully provide you with an even better looking (and working) website.

Unfortunately, hiring someone to create any website worth its salt doesn't come cheap. Sure, there are discount website builders (tons of them), but they only give you what you'd get in option no. 2 by creating a site yourself.

To get a site that looks amazing, is mobile friendly, has good SEO, a good shopping cart, and other tools that make your job easier… we'll, you're probably looking at a minimum of a few thousand dollars.

That's why you need to take time with options number one and two first. Then, you'll know exactly what you want and need from your site so that *when* you can afford it you'll be able to hire the right person.

Advantages of hiring someone to build you a site:

- A professional site enhances your brand image and will enable you to scale up
- A pro might be able to create functionality on your site that you are unable to do yourself
- You save time having someone else do the design and programming for you
- If you don't know what you want, hiring someone else to build it could alleviate stress

(*but note: if you don't know what you want, it will be very difficult to help someone else create the right kind of site for you)

Disadvantages of hiring someone to build you a site:

- A good site comes at a price (usually a steep one).
- It might be challenging to convey your vision for the site to someone else (so the final product won't be what you expect or want)
- You lose some amount of control over your website (how it works, what message it conveys, etc.)

Hiring out a professional makes a ton of sense if you have more money than time, but for most new influencers that isn't the case. Wait to hire until you've grown and are making serious money.

And those are your three options for website development.

The good news is that you can start with option number one (create your own free site) or two (create your own inexpensive site) on a shoestring budget and then make continual upgrades to your website as your web development skills grow or as your budget grows.

There is no reason to wait in creating a blog or a website (basically the same thing)—you can do it today for free.

And you really do see a ton of additional benefits from having that "home base" in order to connect all of the social profiles you will be building, for advertising your services, and for conveying a professional front.

So build a website now. You'll be glad you did.

Build Your Social Media Platform

Once you have a blog or personal website it is then time to create your various social profiles.

You probably already have a few social accounts (e.g. FaceBook, Twitter), but you are using those for personal relationships. Now it is time to create profiles specifically for you as an online influencer.

You can use your personal profiles for your professional life but I highly recommend against that. Don't bombard your friends with your business ideas if you want to keep them as friends... it's really easy just to create new accounts and if your friends *choose* to connect to those accounts that is up to them.

So which social profiles should you set up?

There are so many different social platforms, and new ones are cropping up all the time. So a word of caution...

Don't go crazy here. Set up 2-5 social profiles and then focus on really building up 1-2, at least at first. You're not going to get really big on all of them right away and you'll find with time which platforms work best for you.

Here are a few important questions to consider in selecting your social platforms and in deciding which ones you'll spend your time with:

- Where can you get the most followers fastest?

- Which social platforms do you already use, are familiar with, and like to use?
- Where does your audience hang out?
- Where is the most potential for affiliate sales?

If you don't know the answers to these questions than this is a good place to start. Do a little research and figure things out.

Getting followers fast

One of the most important things I learned early on is that certain platforms make it really easy to get followers while other platforms make it much more difficult.

I also learned that not all followers/ subscribers are created equal. For example, if I post a social mention to 100k twitter followers that were acquired through the "follow back" method (more about that later in the chapter) it is possible that post will only get 5-10 likes and just a couple retweets or shares. Less than 1% (way less) of those followers will click on the product link and I'll be lucky if even one person purchases the product.

However, if I place a one minute unboxing video of the same product to 100k subscribers in YouTube—subscribers who opted-in to the channel because they are looking for particular kinds of products—that single video could result in thousands of dollars in ad revenue, and thousands more in affiliate sales.

What engagement you get on the various social platforms depends upon the value you provide on those platforms.

For example, if a social mention on Twitter simply states what the product is and links to it with a couple hashtags, then it's no wonder the engagement (click through rate) is low. But if a one minute unboxing video on YouTube shows all the best features of that same product—and that product is amazing—then it's no wonder that the click through rate will be much higher.

As a newbie in the product review space I estimate that for me YouTube subscribers are at least 100x more valuable than Twitter followers when it comes to product reviews. But that doesn't mean that Twitter, Facebook, and Instagram audiences don't have their place, especially when you are first starting out and the number of followers you have matters.

But before we discuss how to acquire those followers it is important to point out the difference between casual followers and actual fans.

Followers vs. Fans

Most social platforms (e.g. Facebook, Instagram, Twitter) allow complete strangers to follow you and/or subscribe to your content. Inevitably some of those who "follow" you will simply be "followers" while others may become "fans". Both groups are important to product reviewers, but there are also a few important differences between the two.

"Followers" are simply those who follow you. They are a number. And numbers are important for establishing "social proof" or credibility on most social platforms. If you have 50,000 followers on Twitter, you are much more likely to get free products (or get paid for reviews) than if you have just 1,000 followers. That is true in most cases even if the 1,000 followers are more *engaged* than the 50,000.

Engagement means that the followers make some sort of connection with the content. Generally that means they "like" and "share" the post, and more importantly that they click on the links to purchase the product.

1,000 engaged followers is actually waaaaaaaay better than 50,000 disengaged followers, but many brands don't investigate engagement, they just look for your total audience size. That is their mistake and you can benefit from it early on in your journey. But ultimately you want true fans, not just followers.

"Fans" are engaged. They want to know what you'll review next and they value your opinion on products and brands.

Fans are awesome because they will like, share, and repost your content helping you to expand your audience and reputation. And they do all that without you having to ask them to do so.

While it is relatively easy to attract followers to your social platforms it is much more difficult to obtain true fans. You do that by providing value to them—by helping them make purchasing decisions, informing them regarding the pros and the cons of each product, and by giving them honest and relevant feedback and advice regarding the product.

How to attract followers vs. fans should be common sense, but it isn't talked about very often. When you are establishing a brand and establishing your social presence there is certain value in beefing up your numbers early on. However, the long-term play is to provide real value to your audience in order to attract real fans and grow a legit brand.

To recap: micro-influencers need as many followers as possible as soon as possible. Then, as your brand grows you will try to convert some of those followers to real fans.

You can grow your audience on a single platform or by posting on several. I recommend you get really good at 1-2 first and then branch out if you have the time or feel the need to as you grow.

Below I outline some of the pros and cons of being on and using the most popular social platforms available right now, as well as a few tips on how to quickly acquire followers and how to convert them to fans.

Twitter

Twitter is the social channel that will most likely allow you to get the greatest number of followers in the shortest period of time with the least effort. However, as you now know if you employ a quick-growth strategy most of those followers will likely not be very engaged or likely to purchase your products.

Translation: Twitter can make you look and feel important (because you have a large following) but won't likely help you make a lot of money through affiliate and other sales channels.

The follow-back method. To acquire a sizeable following quickly you probably want to start with the "follow back" method. This method works in other platforms as well but is especially effective in Twitter.

What you do is create a profile and then start following as many people as possible. Some of those who you follow will choose to follow you back. And most of those who follow you back won't unfollow you down the road unless you give them a compelling reason to do so (e.g. you post offensive material or spam them).

So you start by following a ton of people. Then, from time to time you will have to unfollow those who don't follow you back so that you don't follow too many people (Twitter has set limits on how many you can follow without others following you back).

59

This can be a major pain (to unfollow accounts) but fortunately there are tons of free apps and computer programs that can help you unfollow your non-followers with relative ease.

I used the follow back method to gain 5,000 followers in my first month and 35,000 in my first year. That first month I probably spent 1-2 hours a week following and unfollowing others but I got better at it and then spent less time. I now only do this for a few minutes each month (if that).

To get more and better followers try a few of these tips. These are things that work on any social platform but are especially effective in Twitter.

Use hashtags. Post some of the following hashtags on your profile and in your posts: #f4f #followforfollow #followback #l4l #likeforlike. Using these hashtags will make it easier for other people who are growing their audiences to find and follow you.

Follow those who are more likely to follow back. You can find these people by looking at their profiles and seeing how many followers they have and how many people they are following. Look for close to a 1:1 ratio. That indicates that they follow back those people who follow them. I usually try to find someone who has 5-15k followers with a one-to-one ratio and then I follow all of their followers.

Follow people who like products similar to the products you review. So find an influencer in your niche and look at their products. Then follow all of the people who are liking and commenting on their products. This is a good way to get followers who are more engaged and more likely to become fans. Real fans that help you sell products.

Finally, **follow those who engage in related and relevant content**. If you want to start finding those who will be real fans later on and help you with the long-term growth of your channel, you need to look in your niche.

Find posts like yours and see who likes and retweets those posts. Then follow, like, and retweet posts from those people.

Some of them will follow you back and better still they will like and retweet your posts.

These kinds of followers won't find you in droves, but if you can initiate contact and add a few of these quality followers each month it will make a big difference in the long-term.

Facebook

The biggest strength of Facebook is in creating and facilitating a community that is valuable to your audience. By creating a Facebook page for your audience you are giving your readers opportunities to share their own social proof for the products that you are promoting.

I've found that growing a Facebook page for reviews alone is incredibly difficult because there is no inherent community component to reviewing lots of different products. Indeed, most of my "followers" on Facebook are the brands that I am promoting who are lurking on the page to see if anyone else is getting value.

So I wouldn't waste my time setting up and managing a Facebook page unless you have a community you want to grow. That means that there needs to be some coherence in the kinds of products you promote.

If that *is* the case, then set up a page with product reviews for a particular category of products. On that page you should write posts about which of those products are best, what features to look for, how to get good deals, etc. Do that AND find out what your audience wants and deliver that to them.

Basically, you should get to know your audience, learn what they want to know about the products you are reviewing, and answer their questions.

If you provide real value in Facebook then this social channel can be a real benefit to you and your audience.
Finally (and more about this later), Facebook can also be a great place to find companies and brands that you are interested in reviewing for.

Instagram

Instagram (IG) is a visual platform that relies on high quality pictures and quotes to engage an audience. It is a great platform for promoting products because it is so visual.

Instagram works great for unboxing pictures and videos, images of products being used, and staged photos designed to highlight certain features of the product.

You can cultivate an audience in IG much in the same way you do on Twitter—utilizing the follow back method. However, unlike Twitter, IG currently caps the number of people you can follow at 7,500. That means that once you hit that limit your growth relies solely upon the value you provide to your audience.

So while you can grow Twitter into the millions of followers without adding any real value, with Instagram you need to actually provide something worth reading/seeing in order to keep growing.

How do you add value?

First, take great pictures. IG is a mobile-first platform so you'll want to bare that in mind while shooting photos (that most people viewing them will be doing so on their phones).

There are a bunch of filters and photo editing features built right into the Instagram platform so play around with it. You'll find that the more photos you take and post the better you become.

Also, make sure that your product descriptions provide insight into the product and aren't just sales pitches. Let your viewers know the pros and the cons of your products so they can be educated consumers.

Finally, utilize hashtags in your posts. A few years ago the advice was to use as many hashtags as humanly possible. Fortunately, IG figured out this was a bad strategy and now they discourage that practice. Instead use a few targeted hashtags that will actually help your audience.

For example, if you're reviewing a power bank to extend your phone's battery life you might use the hashtags #powerbank, #brandname (the actual name of the brand you are promoting, not "brand name"), and #phonebattery. If you want to see the usefulness of your tags then actually click on them in Instagram and see what they lead you.

Instagram can provide a lot of value in the review space because images can tell a lot about a product. I've found that with a decent following (around 7k) I've been able to get paid for a lot of my IG posts—companies want to have their products on my channel because I take good pictures and post useful descriptions.

It's not too hard to get started with IG and you'll definitely get better the more you post and work on your craft.

YouTube

If you are doing product reviews you need to be on YouTube.

YouTube is a great platform for building an audience—especially in the review space—because video reviews are so effective in reaching the target audience (people who want to buy stuff). If you have a channel that reviews different products then you have a lot of opportunities to market and sell those products.

One of the coolest things about YouTube is that it allows text descriptions to accompany the videos. So if you're marketing a particular product you can actually include a written review as part of the description.

Not only that, but you can link that description to a more detailed review on your blog or website AND include an affiliate link to the actual product.

So there are quite a few different ways to make money on YouTube. The first way that most people consider is through YouTube ads. The problem here is that YouTube keeps changing their barrier to entry in the ads space.

You used to be able to monetize any of your videos, regardless of the size of your audience or the number of views. Then, in 2016, YouTube changed their policy so that you then had to have 10,000 total views on your channel before you could monetize. In 2018, they bumped that up to 400,000 minutes watched and a subscriber base of 1000 subscribers.

Translation: if you don't have a pretty decent sized audience for your YouTube channel (1k or more), you can't make money through YouTube ads (yet).

But not to worry, there are other ways of making money with YouTube.

Currently the easiest way to make money on YouTube is to include affiliate links for your products. So you create a video review and then in the description say something like "click here to buy" and link to an Amazon affiliate link. Then if your audience clicks your link and makes a purchase you'll make a small commission.

If you're doing this through Amazon you're not going to get rich but you can make a few bucks here and there and that will add up.

Don't know how to set up an Amazon affiliate account?

It's actually really easy, especially if you already have an Amazon account (like the kind you use to buy things from Amazon). Just go to https://affiliate-program.amazon.com/ and Amazon will walk you through the steps.

Amazon Reviews

Many brands who find you on Facebook or on a review website will seek you out specifically to do Amazon reviews for them. This is problematic for a number of reasons.

First, it is against the Amazon terms of service to do reviews in exchange for free or discounted products.

That doesn't mean it doesn't happen—nearly all of the top 1000 reviewers on Amazon are getting free products—but it is still technically against their terms of service and may result in you losing your Amazon posting privileges.

Here is what their website says, under "Promotions and Commercial Solicitations":

In order to preserve the integrity of Community content, content and activities consisting of advertising, promotion, or solicitation (whether direct or indirect) is not allowed, including: Offering compensation or requesting compensation (including free or discounted products) in exchange for creating, modifying, or posting content.

So, while you may get great offers from companies for cool stuff that you can review in exchange for the product, it can also result in you getting banned from making any posts on Amazon.

I experienced this first hand. About four or five months into my life as an online reviewer I was told that I could get really cool stuff if I went to Facebook and joined a few Amazon communities there. So I did.

And I did get cool stuff.

After getting added as a "friend" to dozens of foreign Facebook accounts and groups, the solicitations for product reviews started rolling in. Each exchange went down in roughly the same way.

First, they asked if I would review their product with pictures and videos and post it to Amazon reviews. Most often they would ask me to purchase the product at full price so that technically I would be eligible to write a "verified review."

So I'd use my own money to buy the product. It would arrive and I'd take pictures and videos and post the review to Amazon. In most cases I also posted the same videos and reviews to my blog and YouTube channel (repurposing the same content).

Once the reviews were posted the companies would then send me a full reimbursement for the product via PayPal, or in a few cases with Amazon gift cards.

In this way I received about ten remote controlled drones, cars and boats; 6-8 skateboards and long boards, roller skates, nice headphones and Bluetooth speakers, and a few other cool things. Honestly, some of the best products I've reviewed came this way.

But there are/were a few downsides to getting products on Amazon (and Facebook):

One of the biggest pains was "becoming friends" with so many strangers on Facebook. I personally don't like to mix my personal and professional lives on Facebook but you have to if you want to make connections using that platform.

Currently (2018), there is no way on Facebook to become friends or connected to someone who isn't on your personal list of friends. You can create a professional business page, but any interactions you have with people must happen through your general friends list.

Another downside to finding companies to work with on FaceBook is that once you get on a "list" it is very difficult to get off that list. I stopped using Facebook for reviews over a year ago and I'm still contacted regularly from people in Facebook and from others who got my contact information from their friends in Facebook.

One last thing about Facebook…

Just like every other platform, FB can do a lot to help connect you to a specific niche. If you have a small, specialized niche for reviews then this can be very helpful. You can get into groups and be added to lists that cater to that niche.

However, if you are more of a reviewing generalist you'll probably find that the kinds of products you will be able to review through your FB contacts is somewhat limited.

I loved reviewing products found through FB initially because they were products I wanted (drones, athletic equipment, headphones). However, after months of the same people offering me the same products it got pretty old.

While I do still maintain a branded Facebook page I almost never seek out partners on Facebook and I haven't missed out on too much. I think that FB would be more helpful for anyone with a specialized niche.

So find your niche.

Finding Your Niche

Your social following will grow as you create and post more and more useful content and engage your followers. While you can "fake it til you make it" by simply following thousands of others across the various social media platforms, you won't gain an audience that converts (makes purchases) until you start creating useful content.

Most online influencers recommend that you start by "Niching Down".

Niching down means that you are clear about what you want to review, who you want to work with, and who belongs in your audience.

If you are reviewing products on Amazon or on a general review blog then your audience will be wide and general. Even so, if you can "niche down" by selecting a type of product that you review more than others you will be much more likely to attract an engaged audience.

One of the top benefits to niching down is that it makes it easier to sell products. When you are an expert over any given product category your reviews are more meaningful and useful, thereby improving your credibility. When readers believe your opinion based on that experience they are much more likely to make purchases as a result.

You don't have to pick an area right away, I didn't. But as you do more and more reviews you'll probably find as I did that there are certain products that you like getting more than others. Start focusing on those products and you will naturally find your niche over time.

However, a word to the wise... You will quickly find that some markets are more popular or saturated than others. There are pros and cons with doing reviews in an oversaturated or under-saturated market.

Many reviewers want to work exclusively in oversaturated (i.e. crowded) markets because that is where their favorite products are. That might include makeup, technology, or toys. The good news is that there are a ton of products in these categories and if you can establish a name for yourself you can do really well reviewing these products.

The bad news is that everyone else wants to review these same products so it is harder to get good products to review, harder to stand apart from the competition, and harder to establish yourself as an expert.

On the other hand, if you do reviews in very specialized markets (e.g. bicycle lights, kitchen knives, soccer gear) you can much more easily be the go-to guy or gal in that industry. As an expert you can get the fancier high-end products and expand your brand.

The biggest problem here is that you have a much smaller target audience so while there is less competition, there is also less demand (usually).

Whatever niche you choose, start right away in writing and posting reviews. The sooner you start the more quickly you'll establish yourself in any given market.

Chapter 4

Writing Reviews

Creating social posts and writing product reviews is probably a lot easier than you think. There is a bit of a learning curve, but once you get the hang of it you can pretty much create your posts on autopilot.

When I started writing reviews I would agonize over every little detail just to realize months later that most of what I had been doing didn't matter. What does matter?

Quantity.

Whether it is building your brand and social following, making money through affiliate links and advertisements, or simply posting to develop your skills as a writer and marketer, the number one thing that will help you is to...

Post, post, post.

It's crazy to look back at my analytics now to see which posts were the most shared, made the most money, and helped the most people. It's crazy because my top performing posts are definitely not the posts I would have guessed would make it to the top.

For example, one of my top reviews is a how-to guide on installing a shower head. Another is a drone review, but not one of my better drone reviews. Another is a video I made on how to use a laser distance meter.

Not too glamorous. But those posts found an audience and make me money through affiliate links and advertising revenue. And other showerhead, drone, and tool companies have reached out to me to do paid reviews for them.

So how can you predict which of your posts will perform the best?

You can't.

But you can do several small things to increase the chances of having a highly shareable and profitable post.

How to Make a Social Post

As a "social influencer" brands are hoping that you can get their product in front of an audience that will want to buy. That is why niching down and reviewing similar products is so useful.

You often don't need to go to great lengths to promote a product. Simply putting it in-front of your audience often makes a big difference.

If you have a following of 50k people who like dogs and you tweet out a dog leash you just got for review, even without a glowing endorsement there is a decent chance that someone will follow your link and purchase the product. That's because of the 50k dog-lovers there's a good chance that at least a handful are already actively looking for a dog leash. Your post will remind them that they want one, and providing a link makes it easy for them to go ahead and buy.

Now imagine if you have a coupon code for 20% off that same leash. Obviously you would then be much more likely to promote sales. And if you have an affiliate link for that product that can be very good (and lucrative) for you.

If 100 followers use your code and purchase a $20 leash through Amazon, you would receive a 4% commission on each sale, resulting in a 80 cent commission per sale… times 100 = Eighty Bucks! And that's if no one buys anything else on Amazon within 24 hours. More likely your commission would be double or triple that amount.

So a simple social post with the right targeted audience could easily make you $100 or more.

So what is involved in making a simple social post?

1. You need a great picture.

Most social channels rely on great photos to sell products. You don't need a fancy camera to take a great picture—your smartphone will probably work just fine—but there are a few rules/recommendations you should adhere to when shooting for social media:

- *Pay attention to lighting*. If you don't have your own light kit make sure that you have enough natural light and that the light doesn't cast shadows over your product.
- *Keep steady*. If you don't have a fancy tripod you can at least spring $10 to get a small tripod for your

phone. Or you can keep your camera steady by propping it up or against something solid. When your budget allows I do recommend getting a good tripod, especially if you are creating video reviews. A tripod brings consistency, stability, and improved focus to your shots.

- *Arrange a background that won't distract.* I'm constantly amazed at how many products reviewed by newbies feature a messy room in the background. Make sure the product is the star and that there aren't things distracting from it. Most often a simple background of white or neutral grey works best. Find a good backdrop and use it repeatedly. I use my same boring counter for 90% of my product shoots.

- *Take Two.* Try to get two different kinds of shots for each product: a product-only image and an in-context or lifestyle photo. The product-only image will have a simple background and can showcase the product from various angles. The lifestyle photo shows the products being used. These shots tell a story and do very well on Instagram and other social channels.

- **Don't be afraid to touch things up**. This is an area of disagreement among influencers. Some are of the opinion there should be considerable postproduction editing to present as professional a photo as possible. Others (including myself) find that new reviewers are better off doing many quick reviews and just using the best shots that you have. You'll be fine either way.

2. You need a list of the right keywords to use as hashtags.

Keywords are important because they help people who are already searching for your topic. Picking the right hashtags and keywords, however, can be a little tricky because the various social channels use them differently.

For example, it used to be that on Instagram you simply wanted to list as many related hashtags as possible in order to get people to your post. Not so anymore. Instead, using a targeted list of 3-5 relevant hashtags works better.

As a general rule of thumb, use hashtags that will help the right people that don't know about you to find you. In order to do that you have to figure out who your audience is and where they hang out. And to do that you need to follow others in your niche and follow the hashtags they use to see what is being posted.

Spend time getting to know your audience and where they hang out online and you'll find it is much easier to create and share content they want to consume.

3. You need a link to the product.

The whole point of posting a product review is to first inform the audience and then to redirect viewers to a purchase page so they can get the product. The key is to redirect them in a way that also benefits you.

You can do this through simple hyperlinks to the product page or by redirecting your audience to your own blog post or video review. Wherever you redirect your audience, make sure that you use affiliate codes so if they make a purchase you get a commission (more about that on the next point).

Where you redirect your audience depends upon your goals for the review. Are you simply posting an image to Instagram notifying people that there is a sale going on?
If so, then redirect your audience to the product page.

But what if you've been using the product for a while and really want to endorse it?

Then writing a blog post or creating a review video would be more appropriate. With more enthusiasm for a product you are more likely to help your audience make an informed purchasing decision, so give them as much information as you possibly can.

Honestly though, I usually just send my audience wherever the company I'm reviewing for asks me to, and that is determined by how I'm being compensated. If I'm being paid $50 to create a video review then I will post that review on YouTube and then link to it from a shorter review post on Twitter, Instagram, and Facebook.

If a brand is paying me to post an Instagram review, I just write a short review on IG, post an amazing product photo, and redirect my audience to the Amazon product page (through my affiliate link, of course).

Speaking of affiliate links...

4. Use a discount code, an affiliate link, or a personal testimonial whenever possible.

In order to best serve your audience, the brand or company you are posting for, and yourself, you want to make sure everyone is getting as good a deal as possible.

In order to do that you want to always use affiliate links (helps you), discount codes (helps your audience), and utilize personal testimonials (helps the brand).

Affiliate links. As has previously been noted, a great way to monetize your reviews is to use affiliate links when you link to the product. That way the customer gets what they want (often at a discount), you get paid a small commission, and the company you're reviewing for makes a sale.

Most people who want to make money using affiliates start with Amazon because it is so easy to set up an account, and because Amazon is the largest online retailer.

Just go to www.affiliate-program.amazon.com and set up your own account and within days you could be making money by promoting affiliate products. For many reviewers this way of monetizing is much more lucrative than ad revenue generated on your website or the commission you are paid for creating a review.

Of course there are affiliate programs outside of Amazon, but if you get started with Amazon you'll have a good sense of how affiliate marketing works and then you can choose to be an affiliate for others.

Discount Codes. One way to increase the likelihood of your audience clicking on your affiliate link is to provide them with a discount code.

Often the brands you work with will provide you with a discount code without you even having to ask for it. And if they don't, you can ask and they'll often provide a discount for your audience.

Note that discounts usually are time sensitive (for either a set block of time or for a certain number of uses), so let your audience know the details of whatever deal you are making available to them.

Personal Testimonials. One of the best things you can do for your audience is give them a personal endorsement of the product you are reviewing. If you have used it (especially for an extended period of time) and plan to continue using it then your review holds more weight than any other review of someone using the product just one or two times.

Let your audience know how much you have used the product: if you just tried it out once, if you've used it for a week or two, or if you've been using it for years.

If you have that personal experience with a product I recommend you try to write a blog review or do a video review for it. The benefit of these kinds of posts (as opposed to photo only posts on IG, FB, and Twitter) is that they have a lot more detail and they are more useful to your audience. But they also take more work.

So if you do a blog post or a video review you should be able to either get a better product than you'd normally get, or get paid (or paid at a higher rate) than your easier to do product posts.

How to Write a Review

The important thing to remember when writing a review is that the goal is to help the reader better understand the benefits (and disadvantages) of the product so that they will want to make a purchase. The more they purchase the stronger your brand and the more money you make. So...

Make sure you only review products that you are willing to stand behind. Write reviews for products that you want, that you use, that are helpful and make your life better. If you love the product then it will be easy for you to write an effective review that converts your readers into buyers.

If you need a good example of how to write a quality review, simply pick a product that you like and look it up on Amazon. In the customer review section for that product the reviews at the top will have been voted there for being "useful." And that's what you're going for...

Useful.

How do you write a review that is useful? Easy. Simply point out the positive and the negative features from a user standpoint.

- What did you like about the product?
- What did you not like about it?
- Would you recommend it to your friends and family?
- Why or why not?

If you can explain the pros AND the cons of a product the reader will be more likely to trust what you say. Include pictures and video and you have even more credibility. Throw the product up on social media and/or your own blog and you gain social proof.

The best way for an influencer to truly "show" the pros and cons of a product is through video.

How to Film a Review

A lot of people make a lot of money creating video reviews for targeted audiences. Indeed, most of the "YouTube Celebrities" out there are either reviewing video games or products. While you probably won't get rich doing this there are at least three good reasons to create video reviews.

1. Provide additional content to your blog reviews and/or social posts
2. Establish your expertise
3. Make money through affiliate sales and brand deals (sponsored videos)

If you are a product reviewer, than odds are that you have a social platform of choice that you use to showcase your reviews. Whether that be through a blog, Twitter, Instagram, or something else you can benefit by complementing your posts with video content.

Readers like video content because it helps them to visualize the product, and seeing an actual user of the product talk about it provides "social proof."

Utilizing a video to review a product is an easy way to show your expertise in that product category. You can talk about the finer details of the product you are reviewing, but you can also throw in a few details about the category more generally. For example, "this drone has great battery life. It gets 15 minutes per charge while most other drones in this price range get only 10."

When a reader/watcher sees that you know a lot about the product category they will more likely trust your opinion AND they are also more likely to check out your other videos and purchase the products.

Creating a video review is probably a lot easier than you think. It basically includes three parts: 1) shooting A-roll, 2) shooting B-roll, and 3) editing (putting the A-roll and B-roll together).

1. Shooting A-roll. This is the meat of your video. When you're reviewing a product the A-roll depends on what the purpose of your video is (e.g. unboxing, review, comparison) but it will probably include you talking about the pros and cons of the product, and either unboxing the product and showing the various parts and/or you using the product.

A-roll is where I create all my audio and then I shoot B-roll to place on top of the audio to make it more visually appealing.

2. B-roll. B-roll is the "background" stuff that really makes your video stand apart. It can be pictures or videos of your product taken at different angles, zoomed in pictures and videos of various features or labels, and pictures of videos of you using the product.

All of the B-roll is placed on top of the A-roll, so while you're talking on the A-roll it is showing examples and demonstrations from the B-roll.

3. Editing the video. Putting the A-roll and the B-roll together is the hardest part of creating high quality videos. Fortunately there is now a lot of different software that will do this for you. And there are millions of YouTube videos that will show you how to use the various software packages.

So what you need to do first is pick a software program that you want to work with. Common free options include: iMovie (for mac users) and Windows Movie Maker (for PC users). The most common paid software includes Final Cut Pro and Adobe Premiere.

Just get started.

Understanding how great videos are made is nice, but the most important priority early-on is to simply start creating and posting. If that means doing a straight take with no B-roll, that's fine.

CHAPTER 5

Leveling Up

Now that you know why you need to be a social influencer, how to connect with companies, and how to create excellent posts, the question remains...

What do you do with all this cool free stuff?

What to do with all your extra stuff

So what should you do with all that extra cool stuff? Much of what you review is probably stuff that you want or need so getting it for free is obviously saving you a little bit of moo-lah.

Ka-ching!

But the truth is that most of the stuff that you will get is stuff that you don't necessarily need.

I estimate that roughly 10% of the products I received in my first year as a product reviewer were products that I would have bought if I couldn't get it for free. So getting free stuff hasn't really saved me a ton of money.

What it has done is allowed me to upgrade my life in ways I couldn't have anticipated.

Upgrade your Life

I have always owned and needed one or more flashlight. But I have never paid more than $10 to get one because I could never justify the additional expense.

Well, now that I do product reviews and get free stuff I own an $80 flashlight and let me tell you… it is way better than those cheapo $10 ones. The $80 flashlight came with its own batteries and battery charger. It can be used as a lamp and illuminate the whole room, and it can be used as a spotlight to concentrate light in one small area. It's so awesome that it is the same kind that the F.B.I. uses.

You can read my flashlight review on my website or watch it on YouTube. So why do I now own the incredible Solaray ZX-1 flashlight? Because Solaray sent me one. For FREE!

Reviewing products has enabled me to get better versions of things I already have, want, or need. I no longer own the cheapest version of everything but in many cases own the very best of many products.

And it *has* made a difference in my life.

I previously didn't know life could be better with a really good flashlight, an amazing water bottle, premium sheets and towels, etc.

But it is.

Upgrading lots of small things around the house has made home life run a little more smoothly, saved us money in not having to replace cheap products as often, and is just really cool.

Regularly receiving free products has also allowed me to be more generous with others. Of the 400+ products I received in my first year as a reviewer I probably only kept about 100 for myself and my family (I know, that's still a lot of cool stuff). The rest were given away as gifts, to celebrate special occasions, and just because.

Gifting: Birthdays, Holidays, and Other Special Occasions

One of the coolest parts of getting free stuff to review is the exact reason I started reviewing in the first place—so that I could give my kids and others I care about cool gifts. I apply for and review products that I think others will really like and then I store those gifts until the occasion is right to gift.

Now for holidays like Christmas, Easter, Mother's Day, etc. I always have a pile of gifts handy to give to those I care about. Likewise I have weddings, baby showers, and birthday parties covered.

I even have so many gifts stashed away that I have to invent reasons to give stuff away. I've given gifts to celebrate Groundhogs day, to thank people who have helped me with various projects (like moving my piano), and as prizes in an adult Easter egg hunt.

As a school teacher I'm regularly looking for and stashing away products that I think my 5th graders will like. We have class auctions a few times a year using our "honey money" (our classes currency) and the kids bid on the products I reviewed.

They're pretty happy when the reward for working hard at school results in them getting a new drone, headphones, a backpack, a skateboard, or something else that they've always wanted.

Many of my students even "pay it forward" and use their rewards as gifts for others.

But the giving doesn't stop there…

Online Giveaways

Finally, I have found that gifting products to my online audience is a great way of growing my online brand and audience. By creating "give-aways" I can entice my readers to join my newsletter list, like my brand on various social platforms, and/or follow me on those platforms.

Several companies have even offered to give me multiple products specifically so I could keep one to review and give the others away. They will also often provide coupon or discount codes to include in social posts so that all my readers can get the products at a discount.

No matter what you do with the products you review you are adding value to the world by creating the review and most likely you are improving yours and others' lives in the process.

It doesn't matter if you keep those products for yourself, give them to your friends, or give them to strangers. Any way you look at it, it's a win.

CHAPTER 6

Charging for Reviews

It is in a brands best interest to pay influencers for reviews. Research from Sway Group reported marketers who implemented an influencer marketing campaign earned an average of $6.85 in media value for every $1 they spent on paid media.

Brands can easily find micro-influencers to review their products without paying them (in exchange for the product), but those reviews typically aren't as high quality as paid reviews. It's also unlikely that larger influencers (those that actually influence buying decisions) will do a review without some financial compensation.

So your goal as an influencer is to be influential enough that brands WILL WANT to pay you to review their products. This is a win-win for them as you get paid and they sell more products or services.

So the question is how large do you need to be (or how much influence should you have) before you can start asking for paid reviews?

The answer is easy—you should be asking RIGHT NOW!

Even if you only have one follower on one social media platform you want to start getting paid to do reviews because doing paid reviews will motivate you to do better reviews and grow your audience so you can get paid even more in the future.

Later in this chapter I will walk you through how you should be reaching out to brands. But before you ask to get paid, you have to understand what you're worth.

Understanding Your Value

You have to have a general idea of what your influence is worth to a brand or company before you ask them to pay you for your posts.

Then you share that data with brands that will convince them what your influence is worth (you show them how you'll make them money). From there it is easy—they send you money and you promote their products. But how do you come up with that number?

Start by creating a document and listing out all your social platforms. Then, for each platform list the number of followers you have and the average engagement for each post (number of likes, shares, etc.). If you have data on how many people have made purchases based on your recommendations or if you have any audience testimonials make sure to note those down as well.

Many digital marketers adhere to the one cent per follower (or $100 per 10K followers) rule, but only as a starting point for their calculation.

What you can charge depends on a number of factors. The most important metrics that companies are looking for is your audience size (number of followers), amount of engagement your audience has (number of likes, retweets, comments, etc.), your fit with their brand (does your audience by stuff like what they offer), the number of posts, type of post (photo, video, audio, etc.), and where the ad will be promoted.

You can also charge an additional amount if the brand or company wants to use your post in their own promotional materials (on their pages, Amazon product page, etc.).

Micro-influencers typically charge per post whatever the market (companies and brands) are willing to pay. The influencer can then gradually increase their rates as their influence (following) grows.

So at the small side of the spectrum influencers don't charge at all but do product reviews to build their following or in exchange for free or discounted projects.

On the high-end larger influencers typically charge less than $500 per 100,000 followers on Twitter, $1,000 per 100,000 followers on Instagram, $2,000 per 100,000 followers on YouTube, and anywhere from a few hundred dollars to tens of thousands of dollars for sponsored videos or posts.

A good rule-of-thumb is that the more effort required to post (e.g. blog post, YouTube video) the more money you should charge.

My recommendation?

Start high. If you are willing to create a quality product review (on any platform) and help share that review with your social platform(s) you should feel confident in charging brands for those posts.

What do you have to lose? Decide what amount would be fair compensation and then tack on 20% and ask the brand or company for that amount.

But I can sense your concerns… what if you don't have a large audience yet? What if you don't know how to make high quality product reviews? What if you don't know how to ask?

Well you're in luck.

That's why you have this book, right? You should be able to use the earlier chapters to learn how to grow your audience and create quality posts. All that's left is presenting yourself to brands as a true professional that can offer them real value.

To do that you should start with creating and presenting an exceptional media kit.

Creating a Media Kit

What is a Media Kit?

It is essentially a modern and more useful version of a resume or c.v. for content creators (e.g. photographers, bloggers, YouTubers, web designers, online influencers).

What is the purpose of a Media Kit?

To show what you have to offer to potential sponsors, partners, and collaborators. It will tell them how much influence you currently have, exactly what kinds of services you provide, and how much you charge for those services. It can also provide examples of your work and testimonials from those you have worked with in the past.

Putting all this information together in a tight packet is a great way to market yourself to brands and companies. A media kit is important—even for micro-influencers (those with less than 10k followers)—because it is shows you are serious about being an online influencer and it can help you present yourself in a professional manner.

What do you need to include in your Media Kit?

When you create a media kit you should focus on answering three primary questions for your potential sponsor:

- Who Am I?
- Who is my target audience?
- What can I offer you (brands)?

You should craft your answers to those three primary questions by including the following:

- *A headshot.* Make sure it is current and consistent with the profile pictures you use across social media.
- *About Me.* Some sort of "about me" that includes important details about yourself (what you specialize in, what your goals are). You can also list your experience or accolades
- *Contact Information.* Include any of the places you want sponsors to connect with you (email, website, social handles, even physical address, phone)
- *Relevant statistics/numbers.* Number of followers on your various social channels, levels of engagement (average likes, retweets, traffic to blog/website), number of email subscribers, etc.
- *Website stats.* For your website you should include monthly unique visitors, monthly page views, average duration of visit, and bounce rate

- *Audience demographics* (gender, age range, geography)
- *Examples*. Who you've worked with (examples of previous work, current partnerships), thumbnails, links, testimonials
- *What you offer* (sponsorship details, packages)
- *Pricing* (rate sheet, more about this later in the chapter)

What should your media kit look like?

Your résumé is how you present yourself to the world and as the media kit is your influencer résumé you need to make sure that it represents you well and showcases the best of who you are and what you do.

So the design is important. The media kit should give brands a sense of what your reviews and posts look like. Many people hire a designer to ensure their imaging is professional and consistent, but here are a few tips to get you started:

- *Branded header*. Use the same header image in your kit that you use on your website or main social channel(s)

- *Personality*. While it is important that your media kit looks professional, it is also important that it gives a sense of your style and personality. Have fun with it.
- *Consistency*. Please make sure you are consistent with the design you use across your social channels (colors, fonts, etc.). It is very off-putting to see one design represented on one channel and a very different one on another channel. Have a unified front or approach to design.
- White space. While space is your friend. Make sure you let your text breath. When you create a document for presentation it is o.k. to put a little space between lines (like 1.5 spacing) and paragraphs. You also want to give your images space.

Remember that just as your brand with grow and evolve over time, your media kit will continue to grow, evolve, and improve. Don't feel like you need perfection right away. Put down the most important details, get a few images on there, and start using the media kit to build and grow your brand. You can create the media deck using PowerPoint, Slides, or Word... but if you want it to look really good you might consider busting out photoshop or Canva.

How long should the media kit be?

As short as possible while still showcasing what you offer. I recommend you keep it to three pages/slides or less. And one of those pages should probably be your rate sheet.

Creating a Rate Sheet

For my first year or so doing product reviews I was happy just getting free stuff. But as my audience grew and as I acquired more stuff than I needed or even wanted I decided to scale up. So I started doing less free reviews (to simply get the product) and did more paid reviews.

In the beginning I only charged a few dollars and was thrilled when anyone would pay me for something that a few months prior I would have reviewed for free. Most of my reviews would be anywhere from $3-10.

In 2017 (my first year doing reviews) I made $700 for 57 reviews ($12.50 average). Most of those "reviews" were $3 for a social mention and picture on Instagram. But I was able to get about a dozen either blog posts or YouTube videos (or both), and I charged $10-30 each for those.

Add the $700 to the thousands of dollars' worth of product I was receiving and I felt year one was a pretty good one for me. And as my audience grew I was in a better position to charge more for my reviews.

So I raised my rates.

And I decreased the amount of time I spend making reviews. I actually did more paid reviews in year two (96) than I had my first year as a reviewer (57), but I was also able to charge more ($7 for Instagram and $25-35 for videos). Consequently my total for the year in paid reviews ($1081) shows I actually made less per review ($11.25) than I had during year one.

Why?

Because I decided the YouTube videos were too much work for what I was getting paid, so I raised those rates and was more selective for which ones I chose to do. So I made more money overall but also did more reviews, but the reviews I did took much less time. I nearly tripled my return on time for dollars (my dollars per hour).

I was able to work less and make more because my reviews were better, I had a bigger audience with more engagement, and because I had a better sense of how much to charge for a review.

Now I charge $5-15 for a social post that takes me five minutes to make and post, and charge $25-60 for a video (depending on how badly I want the product). And negotiating price has also gotten much easier as I created a rate sheet and media kit.

I've been able to raise my rates, decrease the amount of time I spend making reviews (it's still less than three hours per week), and make more money.

How?

It started with creating my media kit and rate sheet.

So what exactly is a "rate sheet"?

A rate sheet is exactly what it sounds like—a sheet that tells potential business partners how much you charge for goods or services. It is probably the most important component in your media kit.

In the business world nearly all companies have some sort of rate sheet or pricing table. But you're probably just a one-man (or woman) operation just happy to get free stuff. So do you really need one?

Only if you are treating your reviews as a business (…which you should do, so YES you need one).

Let me tell you about how I created my rate sheet to illustrate some of the benefits of having one.

I first created my rate sheet because a company found me through my YouTube channel and asked if I would be interested in creating a video for them in exchange for a cool egg cooker.

I was interested, so I said I would… but then they emailed back and had very specific instructions for not one but ELEVEN videos.

In the past when someone made a ridiculous request I would just ignore the email or write back something like "that's not worth my time".

But this time rather than ignoring them like I was inclined to do, I wrote back and told them that it is unusual that I ever do a YouTube video for free but that I occasionally will do so if I really want the product. I was interested in their product which is why I responded in the first place, but I was now unwilling to do a video without compensation.

They responded by asking "Can you send us your rate sheet"?

At this point as a micro-influencer I didn't know what a rate sheet was or why I was supposed to have one. So I did research and learned that it was simply part of a media kit that shows what I can offer to brands and how I expect to be compensated in return. It took me a few days but I created a rate sheet, using what they were asking for in their videos as a guideline for what to include.

To complete the eleven videos this company had requested I make, I decided to charge slightly higher than my usual rate. I made a sheet that showed my new pricing structure for videos, social posts, etc. I was very specific showing different rates for 1-2 minute videos than 5-7 videos, and basic unboxing videos to premium videos.

Here's a screenshot of a portion of that first rate sheet.

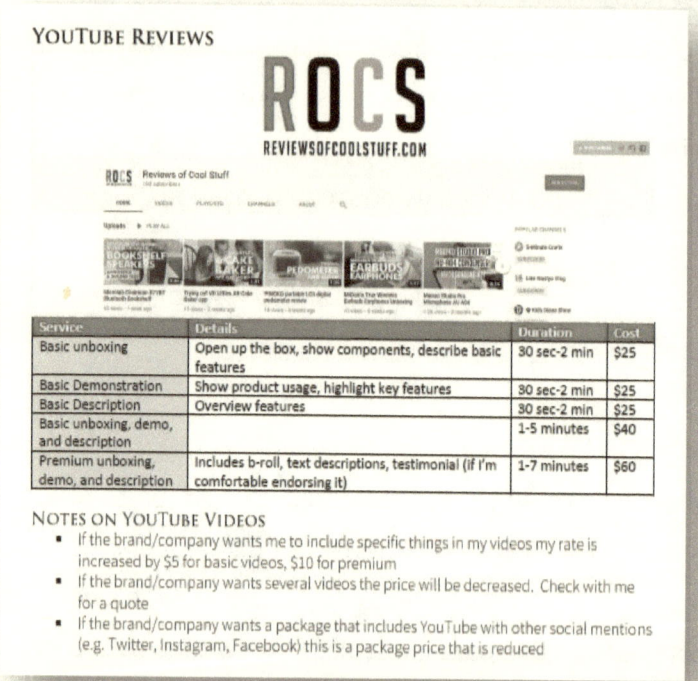

Service	Details	Duration	Cost
Basic unboxing	Open up the box, show components, describe basic features	30 sec-2 min	$25
Basic Demonstration	Show product usage, highlight key features	30 sec-2 min	$25
Basic Description	Overview features	30 sec-2 min	$25
Basic unboxing, demo, and description		1-5 minutes	$40
Premium unboxing, demo, and description	Includes b-roll, text descriptions, testimonial (if I'm comfortable endorsing it)	1-7 minutes	$60

NOTES ON YOUTUBE VIDEOS
- If the brand/company wants me to include specific things in my videos my rate is increased by $5 for basic videos, $10 for premium
- If the brand/company wants several videos the price will be decreased. Check with me for a quote
- If the brand/company wants a package that includes YouTube with other social mentions (e.g. Twitter, Instagram, Facebook) this is a package price that is reduced

My total bill for what they wanted ended up being $270, which would have been way more than I'd ever received for a video review up to that point.

They countered and said they'd hire me for two videos and pay me $85. I was ecstatic. This was still about twice what I was used to getting paid for my video reviews, and for a video that I was originally willing to do for free (with one additional thirty second video).

Not only that, but a few days later another company contacted me and told me they loved one of the pictures I'd posted for them on my Instagram account and asked if they could have that picture to use for their advertising. They had originally paid me $10 to post the picture on Instagram. In the past I would have said given permission to reuse the photo as a way of saying thanks for paying me for my original post.

But now that I had a rate sheet I responded with "I don't give away my creative work without compensation" and attached my rate sheet that showed how much it would cost to use the photo for their own purposes (in this case their Amazon product page).

My rate sheet quoted $25 for use of an image and they didn't even hesitate, I had the money in my account within a few days.

So within a week of creating and using a rate sheet I pocketed a cool $100 that I would not have otherwise received.

What should you include on your rate sheet?

Your services and rates.

It's really as simple as that. It doesn't need to be fancy. Brands just want a ballpark from which they can start price negotiations. Having a rate sheet allows you do that.

What should you charge?

That's a little trickier. Especially in the beginning.

When it comes to reach many people calculate what they should charge according to their CPM or cost to reach one thousand people. For those just starting out a CMP of about $5 is standard. So if you have 10k followers you could/should charge $50, right?

Well, not so fast.

Are your posts actually reaching that many people?

Most social media post aren't viewed by all followers, or even a majority.

How much time does it take you to create the post?

This is how initially I determined what I'll charge. I figured that if I could do a post quickly with minimal editing, then my primary time expenditure would be working with companies to decide what to review, ordering and opening the product, and then following up to get paid after the post.

So for reviewing a hat that cost $10 and I could take a single picture, post it to Instagram with a link to the Amazon page, and not have to do any major editing. And I knock that out in 5 minutes or less. But to order the hat, receive and open the package, and submit the review link to the company once the post is completed... that might take me another 10-30 minutes. So $10 then seems like a reasonable rate.

What I really want, however, is to get either a brand deal (several posts) or for the brand to pay for post across all my platforms (Facebook, Twitter, Instagram, Blog, YouTube). When that happens I can make $50-100 and the time spent on the back end (ordering the product, working with the company) doesn't change too much. So I get paid considerably more for creating the actual posts and will therefore spend more time creating quality posts. This is better for the company and for me.

When I started trying to get paid reviews I started low—too low. The thought was charge $3-5 for a post that will take me 3-5 minutes to create. But that didn't account for the time spent looking for products, for the time ordering and receiving products, or for the time working with brands to make sure I got paid (which could sometimes be a lot).

When I doubled and then tripled my initial rates I found that I was still getting several things to review each week—so I was simply getting paid 2-3 times more for the same amount of work. Now I'm charging even more and accepting less review requests so I have more time to enjoy with my family and other hobbies.

Reaching Out to Companies

So with your social media platforms set up, a website or blog up-and-running, and with a media kit and rate sheet good to go, you're now in a position to start asking for paid reviews.

How do you do it?

Well if all goes well, you won't have to. They'll come to you. I was (and still am) amazed with how many people have contacted me to do paid reviews.

My first several paid reviews were through the Tomoson platform, I just applied for paid campaigns. But as my social platforms grew and as I got better at making reviews, several brands started reaching out to me. They would find me through YouTube, or my Amazon profile, or message me on Instagram or Twitter.

At one point I was getting 20-30 review requests each week. Most of those were not for paid reviews, but a few were. So the challenge became who to say yes to.

Fortunately, having a media kit and rate sheet have helped me decide who to work with. I send interested brands my rates and if they're willing to pay they get back with me and we work together. If they're not then I don't hear back.

If brands aren't beating down your door then you most certainly can reach out to them. And it's easier than you might think.

Decide which products you'd like to review and search for those products on Amazon. Find out who makes or distributes the products and then go to their website and find their contact page. Then just shoot them an email and let them know you're interested in reviewing their products.

Send them your media kit so they know you're legit and let them know how you can benefit them.

So will write back and start a relationship with you. You might have to start with a few free reviews until they see the quality of service you provide, but you'll eventually start getting paid reviews this way.

I recommend you work with small brands as you get started. There are a ton of foreign distributers who are looking for Americans (English speakers) to create product reviews for them. And many of these brands have money in their budgets for marketing. Let them know you're interested and many will jump at the opportunity to work with you.

At the end of the day, the best way to get good gigs is to consistently create great product reviews and market those reviews to your audience. Then, as your audience grows and your reviews improve you will find more and better opportunities.

Of course there are several different ways to grow your brand and find your audience. In the next chapter I'll share some of the things other influencers have done to find success as product reviewers.

CHAPTER 7

Reviewing the Reviewers: What other Influencers Say about Doing Online Reviews

I understand that becoming an online influencer is an individual challenge and your journey won't be the same as mine.

For starters I didn't have a book to guide me through the process... I was truly starting from scratch. But I'm also probably in a niche that is different from yours and have unique skills and abilities that make my experiences unique.

So I reached out to a dozen other influencers to ask them about their journey—how they go started in reviews, what worked for them, etc.

The following Q&A surveys reviewers at different stages of brand growth and development, and across various industries. Each reviewer fielded the same questions but as you'll see the answers vary greatly.

Luciana Batista

(https://www.instagram.com/luciana.peter_1/)

Luciana Batista is an online influencer and product reviewer that reviews a wide array of products, but specializes in makeup, hair, skincare, food, houseware, and toys. You can reach her at her various social channels:

- https://www.instagram.com/luciana.peter_1/
- https://mobile.twitter.com/luciana_peter1
- https://www.facebook.com/luciana.batista.796
- https://www.youtube.com/channel/UC47bny7rRrVvdnJRzKvqX-g

How long have you been reviewing products online and how did you get started? How did you first learn about doing product reviews?

I have been reviewing for four years. I started by looking product reviewing up on YouTube and learned more about how to become a reviewer by searching on social media.

What is the first product that you reviewed?

Pinchme

What is the best product you've ever reviewed? Worst? Best compensation?

I've had so many good reviews. I haven't reviewed a bad product in all these years.

What do you do for a typical review/which platforms do you post to? (e.g. Twitter, IG, YouTube, blog post)

I post to Instagram, Twitter, and Facebook.

How long does a typical review take for you to create, edit, and post? What is the longest amount of time you spent on a review? The shortest?

A typical review is done in a day and the longest I've ever spent working on a review was two days.

What's your number one tip for how to grow an audience on social media?

I use a lot of hashtags like #FollowforFollowback.

What's the one piece of advice you'd give someone considering doing product reviews?

Searching on social media and following big reviewers like Reviews of Cool Stuff

Hollie Newlin

www.hollieshotpicks.wordpress.com

Hollie Newlin is an online product reviewer & influencer. She reviews a wide variety of products with a special interest in skincare, beauty and pet items. She has a B.A. in English from the University of SC. Newlin's hobbies include spending time with her three adorable furbabies, photography, cooking and reading. You can reach her on her blog at www.hollieshotpicks.wordpress.com

How long have you been reviewing products online and how did you get started? How did you first learn about doing product reviews?

I've been reviewing products for a little over two years now. I got started by doing a Google search for "product review sites" and signed up for whatever I could. I also joined some Facebook review groups, which are a great place to learn about how to get started and what makes a good product reviewer.

What is the first product that you reviewed?

Gummy Multi-Vitamins from Social Nature

What is the best product you've ever reviewed? Worst? Best compensation?

The best would definitely have to be my Roku TV! It's awesome & something I use every single day! The worst would be MiraLax laxatives! Not something that's fun to even talk about much less review. Lol. I usually just get compensated with free products but there have been a few companies I've also been paid cash plus free product.

What do you do for a typical review/which platforms do you post to? (e.g. Twitter, IG, YouTube, blog post)

Typical review consists of 300-400 written review plus 1-4 original photos. I post reviews on my website (blog), Instagram, Twitter, Facebook, Facebook page & Pinterest.

How long does a typical review take for you to create, edit, and post? What is the longest amount of time you spent on a review? The shortest?

I always take the time to thoroughly test & research every product I review. I spend about 4 to 5 hours doing the actual review including writing the review, taking photos & editing everything. If photos aren't needed, it usually takes an hour or two depending on the product.

What's your number one tip for how to grow an audience on social media?

In order to get active followers - meaning ones that like & comment on your posts, you've got to return the support & do the same for their posts. Also always be friendly & helpful if anyone has any questions about a product you've posted about.

What's the one piece of advice you'd give someone considering doing product reviews?

You must be willing to put in the time & effort in order to be a successful product reviewer. Sometimes I spend 14 hours a day reviewing, applying for products to review, taking photos etc. It's a full time commitment.

Rebecca Gisborne
@rebeccarosereviews

Rebecca Gisborne is a writer and reviewer/influencer at @rebeccarosereviews. While being open to reviewing many products, but especially chocolate, she specializes in beauty. The main focus of her page is beauty and poetry, and a general unleashing of her creativity on the world. Ultimately, her job will be monetizing her page, so that an ever growing number of people can appreciate her genius. She loves history, art and anything French. You can reach her at @rebeccarosereviews on Instagram.

How long have you been reviewing products online and how did you get started? How did you first learn about doing product reviews?
I've been reviewing products online for about a year and a half. I started through 'insta-blogging' (writing short, blog like posts on Instagram).

What is the first product that you reviewed?
The first product I ever got sent to review for free was a pink clay face mask.

What is the best product you've ever reviewed? Worst? Best compensation?

The best compensation I ever received was through a sock company, who sent me a lot of socks and underwear. Thankfully, I haven't received a 'worst' product yet. One of the best things I received was essential oils and a diffuser because they were packaged so beautifully.

What do you do for a typical review/which platforms do you post to? (e.g. Twitter, IG, YouTube, blog post)

I post to Instagram. I'll research the product and company, use it over a period of time, and photograph the product. The process varies, depending on the product, what the company wants, etc. If I have any doubts, I'll email them.

How long does a typical review take for you to create, edit, and post? What is the longest amount of time you spent on a review? The shortest?

I usually take quite a while for reviews, but it varies considerably. The process of photographing, editing the photos, writing the review, researching the product, interacting with the company, etc., takes time. I usually like to post as promptly as possible though. I try to take a maximum of two weeks from when I receive a product to post the review.

What's your number one tip for how to grow an audience on social media?

Be genuinely interested in engaging with and supporting other people. Be authentic, and put out high quality content.

What's the one piece of advice you'd give someone considering doing product reviews?

Work hard at it, and approach the task with integrity when it comes to both your followers and businesses supporting you. Value your followers, because you can get nowhere without them.

Trisha Lynn Koch
@Tlynnreviews

Trisha Lynn Koch is an online micro-influencer and product reviewer. She reviews a wide range of products from skincare to electronics. Her day job is as a Certified Nurse Aide, and loves to spend time with her 5 year old son, and boyfriend of 2 years. She is from a small town in Pennsylvania. You can reach her on Instagram @tlynnreviews.

How long have you been reviewing products online and how did you get started? How did you first learn about doing product reviews?
I've been reviewing products online for about 3 years. This past year, I've put more time and effort into reviewing products! When I was 18 I had joined a few websites that would offer samples to try. I had joined a few more sites that offered samples, but reviewing the samples was a requirement. I liked reviewing products, so I decided to post on social media too!

What is the first product that you reviewed?
The first product I reviewed was a face cleanser/mask from Neutrogena.

What is the best product you've ever reviewed? Worst? Best compensation?

The best product I've ever reviewed was my fitbit charge 3! The worst products that I've reviewed is definitely the SeneDerm Skincare Line by SeneGence. As far as compensation goes, I don't normally get paid for it. I'm totally fine with receiving the products as compensation! I have received $5 USD for 1 Instagram post. I hope to one day receive monetary compensation also!

What do you do for a typical review/which platforms do you post to? (e.g. Twitter, IG, YouTube, blog post)

I do reviews on panel websites, Influenster, 08liter, etc. I also do reviews on retailer websites such as Amazon, Walmart, Target, Ulta, and more. When doing social media reviews, I post to Instagram [@Tlynnreviews] , twitter, Facebook, and will soon do YouTube!

How long does a typical review take for you to create, edit, and post? What is the longest amount of time you spent on a review? The shortest?

I typically spend about an hour and a half to create, edit, and post. The longest time it took for a review was about 3 hours, to get a great photo and write the actual review. The shortest time took about 10 minutes, but you could tell I didn't put much thought or effort into it.

What's your number one tip for how to grow an audience on social media?

My #1 tip on how to grow an audience on social media would be two things actually.. Creating fun/interesting content, and interacting with your followers!

What's the one piece of advice you'd give someone considering doing product reviews?

It takes a lot of time to do! You don't want bad quality pictures, and you also need to put thought into your review! You don't need a huge following to do it, you have to start somewhere, right?

Heather Bursey

burseygirl84@yahoo.com

@burseygirl84reviews

.

Heather Bursey Alvelo is a stay-at-home mom, Brand ambassador, product reviewer, and social media influencer. She reviews a big variety of items from coffee mugs, to toddler bikes. She loves spending time with her family, doing arts and crafts, drawing, painting, couponing, and trying to help others in any way she can. You can reach her at burseygirl84@yahoo.com or @Burseygirl84reviews on Instagram. Please feel free to contact her with any questions or feedback

How long have you been reviewing products online and how did you get started? How did you first learn about doing product reviews?

I have been reviewing for almost 3 years. I joined smiley 360 and buzz agent, and then I saw people getting free stuff for reviewing it online, like on Facebook and Instagram. I thought that was pretty sweet so I did a whole bunch of research and found some sites and slowly joined them. I then found of bunch of people who did similar things and they introduced me to other sites.

What is the first product that you reviewed?
The first product I ever reviewed was tea bags. It was from a company on Tomoson

What is the best product you've ever reviewed? Worst? Best compensation?
That's a tough one. I have really been blessed with reviewing some pretty awesome stuff. I really loved the toddler bike I got my daughter for 70 cents!

The worse thing I reviewed was probably a body waxing kit. It's didn't work and burned me. I haven't had a lot of luck in the compensation department, but I do get some paid content distributions on Tomoson sometimes. That is pretty much advertising a brand worthy reviewing it but getting paid to post. I made $20 on a few of them.

What do you do for a typical review/which platforms do you post to? (e.g. Twitter, IG, YouTube, blog post)
I post on my personal Facebook, my Facebook page, twitter, Instagram and YouTube the most. I also blog sometimes about the products I review.

How long does a typical review take for you to create, edit, and post? What is the longest amount of time you spent on a review? The shortest?

I typically take a bunch of pictures at different angles, edit, and slowly add things to my word pad on my phone. Things that I like about it etc. Then I put it all together when save review it many many times then I post. I think I actually spend too much time on my reviews but I'm so happy that I get these items so cheap that I feel I owe it to the seller. I spend less time on thing like coffee mugs, perfume, toothbrushes because there is only so many things you can say about a cup. So longest would be 2 weeks, shortest 3 days

What's your #1 tip for how to grow on social media?

I try to find people that have the same interests, and other reviewers. I try to keep my stuff unique and different from anyone else's stuff. I love to be different

What's the one piece of advice you'd give someone considering doing product reviews?

Just because you get it dirt cheap or free doesn't mean you don't have to work for it. It's not as easy as it sounds. But I personally enjoy it and plan to review even when I'm 80!! I love it.

McKay
http://www.gotechgeek.com/

McKay spends most of his day doing IT for a tech startup. When he comes home he enjoys spending time with his beautiful wife and two cute boys. When everyone else is sleeping though (usually early in the morning), McKay enjoys having the opportunity to test and review many tech items. Visit his YouTube https://www.youtube.com/c/GoTechGeek or website http://www.gotechgeek.com/ or for more info.

How long have you been reviewing products online and how did you get started? How did you first learn about doing product reviews?
I started in the fall of 2015. I found out about reviewing products because my younger brother had a couple companies send him free items to review. I contacted those companies along with a handful of other companies and discovered a couple online sites that helped facilitate reviews.

What is the first product that you reviewed?
Mpow armband phone holder for jogging.

What is the best product you've ever reviewed? Worst? Best compensation?

Best: Halo Rover. At the time this cost over $700. To date I have received over $3000 either directly or indirectly from reviewing that. Worst: A solar light. It worked great for a few days, then all of a sudden it blew up. It literally exploded and left a black mark on my fence. If anyone in my family would have been near it at the time they could have been severely injured.

What do you do for a typical review/which platforms do you post to? (e.g. Twitter, IG, YouTube, blog post)

I do almost exclusively YouTube videos. My goal is to show the pros and cons of the item in as little time as possible.

How long does a typical review take for you to create, edit, and post? What is the longest amount of time you spent on a review? The shortest?

I spend probably about 3-5 hours on most reviews. I usually spend about 1-2 hours getting video footage of the item, 30 minutes to record me talking about it, then 1-2 hours for me to put the video footage together and post it on YouTube. Hard to say what the longest time I have spent on a review; probably around 12-15 total hours. Shortest: Probably about one hour for a super simple product.

What's your number one tip for how to grow an audience on social media?

For YouTube I would say to create something that has a unique element to it that is different from other videos. Have your video be high enough quality that most viewers feel compelled to watch the entire video.

What's the one piece of advice you'd give someone considering doing product reviews?

Do it because you enjoy it and don't set your expectations too high. It is a LOT of work if you want to make money and there is a good possibility that you won't make money. If you are not enjoying it, then it is not worth it.

Lauren Lorenz
@laurenreviewsit

Lauren Lorenz is an outgoing, fun-loving mother of three that enjoys reviewing and promoting products for everyday life. You can find her on Instagram @laurenreviewsit to check out her most current content.

How long have you been reviewing products online and how did you get started? How did you first learn about doing product reviews?
I have been reviewing products off and on for about 4 years. I got started after reading an article online that I stumbled across, and just kinda became hooked.

What is the first product that you reviewed?
I really don't remember now, sorry!

What is the best product you've ever reviewed? Worst? Best compensation?
The best thing I ever reviewed was the entire line of Drunk Elephant's skin care products. The worst would probably be this weird herbal weight loss tea. It tasted horrible! So far my best compensation has been about $150, but I have really

just recently started taking it seriously as a business endeavor, prior to that I just did it as a hobby.

What do you do for a typical review/which platforms do you post to? (e.g. Twitter, IG, YouTube, blog post)
I post to Instagram, Twitter and Facebook. I recently started a YouTube channel and a blog, but I have not utilized them so far. Primarily, Instagram.

How long does a typical review take for you to create, edit, and post? What is the longest amount of time you spent on a review? The shortest?
A typical review takes me about a week from the time I receive the product. I like to have time to experience the product and get a good feel for it so that I can post more detailed reviews. The longest amount of time spent was a month, but that was because of the type of product I was reviewing. I needed to log results over time before I could properly review the product.

What's your number one tip for how to grow an audience on social media?
Engage with other people in your topic. If you post makeup related content then reach out to other people that post makeup related content and like, follow and comment.

Odds are they'll do the same in turn and before too long you have a genuine, active audience base.

What's the one piece of advice you'd give someone considering doing product reviews?
Be creative. Try to post unique photos with your content and be descriptive in your review.

RD Drone Reviews
rdevall71@gmail.com

RD's Drone Reviews is a YouTube channel devoted to unbiased reviews of remote control products with a focus of drones. He tries to provide thorough and honest reviews so buyers know what r/c products are worth spending their hard earned money on.

How long have you been reviewing products online and how did you get started? How did you first learn about doing product reviews?
Two and a half years. I got started reviewing r/c products because a friend who reviewed owed me a favor so he connected me with a sponsor and the rest is history.

What is the first product that you reviewed?
The first free product I reviewed was the JJRC H31 quadcopter.

What is the best product you've ever reviewed? Worst? Best compensation?
Best would be the Autel EVO. The best free product would be the DHK Maximus. The worst was the Ja Ding Toys "Inspire" clone drone.

What do you do for a typical review/which platforms do you post to? (e.g. Twitter, IG, YouTube, blog post)

YouTube is where I post my videos then I share them to Facebook, Reddit and RC groups.

How long does a typical review take for you to create, edit, and post? What is the longest amount of time you spent on a review? The shortest?

Most take me 2 hours you film and edit. That longest would be 5-6 hours for the Evo review.

What's your number one tip for how to grow an audience on social media?

Don't be afraid to pay a little cash (YouTube, Facebook, etc.) to advertise your content.

What's the one piece of advice you'd give someone considering doing product reviews?

Be patient, it takes time to grow an audience.

Cynthia Sosa
@calireviewingmama

Cynthia Sosa is an online product promoter and influencer. Head to her Instagram @calireviewingmama to see her beautiful pictures and honest reviews.

How long have you been reviewing products online and how did you get started? How did you first learn about doing product reviews?

I have been reviewing products since April 2014, so 4 years. I got started with couponing. I wanted to share my deals and hauls to help others. I learned about reviewing products when I discovered Influenster, an online source of honest reviews.

What is the first product that you reviewed?

The first product or should I say products because it was an Influenster Voxbox that included 5 products. Suave Moroccan Infusion Shine Styling Oil with Argon Oil, Olay Fresh Effects Shine, Shine Go Away! Shine Minimizing Cleanser, Dr. Scholl's For Her High Heel Insoles, Goody Tangle Fix Detangling Brush, and NYC New York Color Liquid Lipshine.

What is the best product you've ever reviewed? Worst? Best compensation?

The best product I've reviewed would hands down be SheaMoisture's African Black Soap, it helped me be confident and love my skin again. The worst product I've tried would be L'Oréal Paris 10% Pure Vitamin C Serum. My forehead and cheeks started to itch. I got little bumps all over my forehead and a few on my cheeks.

What do you do for a typical review/which platforms do you post to? (e.g. Twitter, IG, YouTube, blog post)

I post on all my social medias, which includes Instagram, Facebook and Twitter. However, I'm more active on Instagram. It's my biggest influential platform.

How long does a typical review take for you to create, edit, and post? What is the longest amount of time you spent on a review? The shortest?

I'm a perfectionist, so getting the perfect picture or video can take a while. Then I do edit and make sure it comes out even more beautiful. I usually take about two hours because I also like to thoroughly write my reviews. Video content obviously takes way longer and can be frustrating, I can't recall exactly how long it takes but I'll estimate to four hours since my videos aren't long. Shortest time I've spent an hour. When I happen to get a perfect picture in the first few shots and it doesn't need much editing.

What's your number one tip for how to grow an audience on social media?
My number one tip for growing an audience would be to show love and support to other amazing influencers. We all want loyal and supportive followers, who truly want to know our opinion.

What's the one piece of advice you'd give someone considering doing product reviews?
Don't let the numbers get to you. Whether it's followers, likes or/and comments. It takes lot of time and hard work to finally see progress. Don't give up, you can achieve anything.

Products-samples-reviews

How long have you been reviewing products online and how did you get started? How did you first learn about doing product reviews?
I started reviewing products 5 years ago. I received private email invitations from companies, that's how I got started.

What is the first product that you reviewed?
Facial oil for skin chemist's

What is the best product you've ever reviewed? Worst? Best compensation?
Advanced mixology are the best products, I'm always compensated in full.

What do you do for a typical review/which platforms do you post to? (e.g. Twitter, IG, YouTube, blog post)
I only post personal reviews on my Instagram. I also post reviews on amazon, numerous company websites.

How long does a typical review take for you to create, edit, and post?
Most of my reviews take 15 mins. I've had to spend a half hour on a few that needed more details.

What's your number one tip for how to grow an audience on social media?
Be honest, respectful & supportive!

What's the one piece of advice you'd give someone considering doing product reviews?
Be honest, friendly, and informative & enjoy doing it!

Samantha Bundy
www.samanthatownsend.com

Samantha Bundy is an online blogger and influencer. She specializes in travel and reviews of beauty and self-care products. She works as a summer camp director and loves traveling whenever she can. You can reach her by visiting her website www.samanthatownsend.com or on Instagram @myproducts13

How long have you been reviewing products online and how did you get started? How did you first learn about doing product reviews?
2 years. Saw an ad for Influenster on Instagram.

What is the first product that you reviewed?
Tresseme shampoo

What is the best product you've ever reviewed? Worst? Best compensation?
Worst: cinnamon chips Best: Joah cosmetics

What do you do for a typical review/which platforms do you post to? (e.g. Twitter, IG, YouTube, blog post)
Instagram

How long does a typical review take for you to create, edit, and post? What is the longest amount of time you spent on a review? The shortest?
5-30 minutes

What's your number one tip for how to grow an audience on social media?
Consistent posts

What's the one piece of advice you'd give someone considering doing product reviews?
Don't be afraid to offer to review products. Worst they can say is no

ACKNOWLEDGMENTS

Writing this book has been a privilege. I am grateful that when times were tough for me and my family that going online to get free stuff was actually an option.

I'm super appreciative to my brother McKay for encouraging me to check out Tomoson and look into doing online reviews, something he had been doing for some time. He encouraged me along the way, and mentored me through the process. I couldn't have done this without him.

And another thank you to others who have supported and encouraged me along the way. My other brother Dallin and my parents have been my cheering section, and my students have been good to say thank you when they get stuff in our classroom auctions.

Thank you to the contributors to this book who shared their own experiences: Luciana, Hollie, Rebecca, Trisha, Heather, McKay, Lauren, RD Drone guy, Cynthia, Product Samples gal, and Samantha. Your insights show that there are so many different ways to have success as micro influencers.

Thank you to my students at GWA. It is such a privilege to teach you and see you grow and develop. I'm so grateful to be able to reward you for your hard work from time to time with the free stuff I get as an online reviewer. I wish I could do more.

The biggest thank you goes to my amazing wife Natalie and our four exceptional kids. Thank you for putting up with me getting stuff all the time ☺. While I know you like the free stuff we get, I also recognize that most of that stuff goes to other people (as gifts or to my students).

So thank you for tolerating the empty Amazon boxes, the endless pile of things to review (we store them in the kitchen), and the 2-3 hours each weekend that I give to others instead of spending my time with you. You are rock stars and mean the world to me.

Finally, thank you to the readers of this book. I hope this is able to help and guide you to getting free stuff that will improve your life and the lives of those around you. I'll keep posting what I learn about being an influencer on my blog and YouTube channel, so feel free to visit me there.

ABOUT TYLER

Tyler Christensen & Reviews of Cool Stuff

Tyler Christensen is a husband, father, teacher, web designer, online influencer, sports writer, YouTuber, blogger, DIYer, marathon runner, and musician. He's a busy dude.

He started the product review website Reviews of Cool Stuff (www.reviewsofcoolstuff.com) December 2017 because he wanted to get his kids cool stuff for Christmas but he was unemployed and couldn't afford to buy cool things (or even uncool things).

Tyler followed the advice of his brother and started applying for products on the website www.tomoson.com and was surprised to get accepted for several things in the first month—even with a pitifully small social following.

In 2018 he reviewed more than 400 products (worth more than $5k) and got paid nearly $1,000 because some of those reviews were paid reviews.

Tyler has never spent more than five hours a week doing reviews or review-related activities (like growing social media audience, taking and posting pictures, or writing review posts) but continues to get free stuff all the time.

Now he gets paid for most of his posts and he gives away most of the products. It's a good gig for a busy school teacher.

Tyler sometimes talks about himself in the third person (like when he submits his bio for a book) but the rest of the time he's just an ordinary dude.

You can learn more about him and his various projects at: www.tylerchristensen.com or more about his reviews at: www.reviewsofcoolstuff.com or on his YouTube channel at: https://www.youtube.com/c/ReviewsofCoolStuff.